creative
ACTIVITIES FOR
Plot, Character & Setting

TERESA GRAIN
KATHY GOOU
ANDREW LAM

AGES 5-7

Authors
Teresa Grainger,
Kathy Goouch and
Andrew Lambirth

Editors
Clare Gallaher and
Victoria Lee

Assistant Editor
Charlotte Ronalds

Series Designers
Anthony Long and
Joy Monkhouse

Designer
Helen Taylor

Illustrations
Mark Oliver

The publishers would like to thank:

The staff and pupils at **Hextable Infant School** and **Hextable Junior School**.

Helen Nokes and her pupils at **St James Infant School**.

The authors would like to thank all the energetic and creative professionals on the Advanced Certificate in Creativity in Literacy Learning, and the Masters courses in Language and Literacy who have trialled these ideas in their classrooms; all the talented children who supplied work included in this publication.

Published by Scholastic Ltd,
Villiers House,
Clarendon Avenue,
Leamington Spa,
Warwickshire CV32 5PR

www.scholastic.co.uk

Text © 2004 Teresa Grainger, Kathy Goouch and Andrew Lambirth
© 2004 Scholastic Ltd

Designed using Adobe Indesign

Printed by Belmont Press, Northampton

2 3 4 5 6 7 8 9   4 5 6 7 8 9 0 1 2 3

British Library Cataloguing-in-Publication Data

A catalogue record for this book is available from the British Library.

ISBN 0-439-97111-X

The rights of Teresa Grainger, Kathy Goouch and Andrew Lambirth to be identified as the Authors of this work have been asserted by them in accordance with the Copyright, Designs and Patents Act 1988.

Contents

4 **Introduction**

Chapter One:
Story Structure

7   Introduction
10 Three seeds of story
12 Story hands
14 Story bags
16 Stories in sound
18 The story cauldron
20 Stepping stones to cross the river
22 Story journey scrolls
24 Story boxes
26 Change the ending

Chapter Two:
Characterisation

29 Introduction
31 Adopting roles
32 Hot-seating
34 Thought-tracking
36 Will you be my friend?
38 I need a home
40 Characters in the family
42 Character ladders
44 Understanding Mister Wolf
46 Character pockets
48 Shaking out characters

Chapter Three:
Story Settings

49 Introduction
52 Through the magic mirror
54 Making story worlds
56 Drawing a setting
58 Picture poems
60 Photographs
62 Let's make the place
64 Place the story

Chapter Four:
Theme and Language

65 Introduction
68 Book-spread
70 Mirror the theme
72 Speaking out
74 Advertise the film
76 Songs, rhymes and chants in stories
78 'Get out of here'
80 Washing lines
82 Telling together

Stories to Tell

86 Wee Meg Barnileg
88 The Big Wide-mouthed Toad-frog
90 The Wrestling Animals
92 Sun Frog and Moon Frog
94 How the Tides Came to Ebb and Flow

Introduction

Stories play a central role in early literacy learning; they invite children to dwell in their imaginary worlds and encourage them to make connections between texts and their own lives. Between the ages of five and seven, children are building on their early encounters with significant narratives and becoming more aware of stories both as a source of pleasure and as artefacts made with words. In the process of playfully engaging with texts, re-enacting them and retelling them, young learners become more aware of the structure of stories, the characters who inhabit them and their settings, themes and story language. Documents for the Foundation Stage, the National Curriculum and the National Literacy Strategy all highlight the enjoyment and learning which can be achieved through a focused engagement in story narrative and its elements. This engagement is the focus for this book.

Teachers know that to be effective they need to develop the literacy curriculum creatively and in response to the needs and interests of their young learners. Such an approach seeks to profile texts of all kinds, particularly story narratives, regardless of whether they are found in the realms of picture book texts, oral stories, comics, short novels, television programmes, films, even on CD-ROM and in computer games.

Quality stories motivate and involve young learners and provide powerful fictional contexts for developing understanding about print, and making use of their word, sentence and text-level knowledge. Making the most of such tales provides a real purpose for learning to read and they deserve to be given a significant role in literacy learning.

Creative Activities for Plot, Character and Setting Ages 5–7 is the first in a trio of books on creatively teaching story elements across the primary years, facilitating children's creative involvement with the meanings and pleasures of narrative texts. All books respond to the requirements of the National Curriculum, as well as the recommendations in the National Literacy Strategy, and focus on creative and flexible strategies which teachers can adapt and transform for themselves.

The books are based on the belief that effective teachers of literacy are informed and creative teachers of literacy, teachers who build strong relationships, know about language and learning and are responsive to learners' needs. They are teachers who are able to inspire and motivate children to ensure deep and meaningful learning. Such teachers create imaginative contexts for

purposeful literacy use and make full use of open-ended literacy activities, as well as employing direct instruction when appropriate.

The wealth of interactive activities offered in this book are intended to support teachers in developing more exploratory approaches to narrative. There are no formulas here, no panaceas, but a bias towards the innovative is evident, and playfulness and imaginative engagement are actively encouraged. In enabling children to explore stories 'from the inside out', and to journey into the unknown with their teacher, the activities celebrate the critical role of creativity in the process of literacy learning.

Teachers are invited to experiment with the suggested activities, and to take a full part in them, responding with and to their learners and adapting the ideas flexibly to suit. In adopting more creative approaches, both you and the children will be involved in the generation of imaginative story ideas and the evaluation of these ideas, and this will enrich the children's understanding of narrative elements in the process.

The range of possible narratives

At home and at school, in clubs, the cinema and the library, young children meet a wealth of narrative forms. The stories they hear in school will often be in Big Book format although ordinary sized picture books will also be extensively used.

The National Literacy Strategy appropriately highlights the following stories and rhymes for working with children in Years 1 and 2 (Primary 3 and 4): those with predictable and repetitive patterns; traditional stories; fairy stories; stories with familiar, predictable and patterned language from a range of cultures; stories about fantasy worlds; stories with familiar settings; extended stories; stories by significant children's authors; and different stories by the same author. All the example texts chosen for use in this book and commented on in 'Literature links' are texts drawn from this repertoire.

Knowledge of quality children's literature is central to the practical strategies offered here, which is why suggestions have been made in 'Literature links' which are appropriate to each activity. Mostly, however, the activities can be applied to almost any story text in almost any form, although picture fiction and traditional tales are the easiest and most efficient to use at this and later key stages. These stories are usually short and demonstrate their structure in a more overt manner, and as such act as appropriate models for young readers and writers. Teachers, too, will have favourite books which they know will engage their particular children.

To honour the text and the children's interests, multiple readings of the particular story will be needed to enrich the children's ability to identify, engage with and comment upon, textual features. Such re-readings will also offer considerable pleasure as the children get used to the patterns and rhythms of stories, which become well known and well loved.

		P			
		U			P
		R			L
		P			E
		O			A
B	**A**	**S**	**I**	**C**	**S**
A	U	E	N	R	U
L	T		T	E	R
A	O		E	A	E
N	N		G	T	
C	O		R	I	
E	M		A	V	
	Y		T	I	
			I	T	
			O	Y	
			N		

Revisiting the basics in literacy learning

In recent years the pressures of accountability and targets have arguably narrowed provision in the primary phase. However, the Foundation Stage curriculum makes clear that a more playful, child-centred early learning agenda and good practice in Key Stage 1 should be the building blocks for later work. Teachers and practitioners in the early years know that quality literacy learning involves the integration of reading, writing, speaking and listening, and ensures that the child is imaginatively engaged in their own learning. The 'basics' are worth restating to ensure literacy provision is rich and well balanced.

The activities in this book are formed upon such basics and respond in particular to the new QCA speaking and listening objectives. Activities in 'Moving on' are also offered, which teachers can select from and, through interaction with the children, shape to their needs.

© Thinkstock

Chapter One

Story Structure

p10	Three seeds of a story
p12	Story hands
p14	Story bags
p16	Stories in sound
p18	The story cauldron
p20	Stepping stones to cross the river
p22	Story journey scrolls
p24	Story boxes
p26	Change the ending

Structure is a significant story element and needs to be noticed, experienced, discussed and constructed at both the Foundation Stage and Key Stage 1.

Through inhabiting fictional worlds in make-believe play, listening to the teacher reading aloud, and participating in joining-in sessions and oral storytelling, young learners can become more aware of the structure of a story. Initially, this awareness will be implicit, but through a range of activities, which may include drawing, playing with toys and story props, making small story worlds, retelling tales and role-play, their explicit knowledge of story structure can be developed.

Young children need to actively voice stories and experience their verbal patterns and big organisational shapes through storytelling and dramatic engagement.

© 2001 Creatas

The National Literacy Strategy profiles a number of aspects of narrative structure for children aged five to seven. These include becoming aware of the structural language patterns often found at the start and at the close of traditional tales (for example, *Once, many years ago, in a land far from here...*), as well as the repetitive language patterns within a story which help to shape the structure (*Run, run as fast as you can... Fee, Fi, Fo, Fum...*). The 'Stories to Tell' section in this book contains many examples of these.

Children are also expected to be able to divide stories into beginnings, middles and ends and make use of these elements in their retellings and in structuring their own writing. Tales such as *We're Going on a Bear Hunt* by Michael Rosen and *Owl Babies* by Martin Waddell (both published by Walker Books) have a clear story structure and can be used to retell, as well as to discuss, reasons for incidents in stories.

In addition, children will be involved in identifying the key points of a story in sequence and representing plot outlines using pictures, objects, diagrams and so on. It is clear that time needs to be spent acquainting children with highly structured stories and engaging them with the organisational patterns of such stories, in order to identify the stages of a tale's telling.

Key Stage 1 children need to be aware that their own written stories must contain events and actions which shape the narrative and influence the characters. Their own tales can also be used as a basis for telling and retelling, recording or writing stories which are linked to familiar incidents in well-known tales, for example, losing a favourite toy as in *Dogger* by Shirley Hughes (Red Fox) or being afraid of the dark as in *Can't You Sleep, Little Bear?* by Martin Waddell (Walker Books).

A wealth of story structures exist and some are noted below with accompanying lists of popular Key Stage 1 stories, many of which are in Big Book form. Numerous others pertinent to later activities in this chapter are also noted in the 'Literature links' sections, although other known texts will obviously be worth examining.

Problem resolution tales

These tales are common and often introduce a problem early in the story and then a number of steps are taken to resolve the situation. Using 'Story hands' (see page 12) is one way to notice the structure of problem resolution tales, and 'Change the ending' (see page 26) can also be employed to examine alternative endings. Stories in this category include:

- **'Wee Meg Barnileg'** (a traditional tale on page 86)
- *The Rainbow Fish* – Marcus Pfister (North–South Books)
- *What Made Tiddalik Laugh* – Joanna Troughton (Puffin)
- *The Boy Who Lost His Belly Button* – Jeanne Willis (Red Fox)
- *Owl Babies* – Martin Waddell (Walker Books)
- *Do Little Mermaids Wet Their Beds?* – Jeanne Willis (Andersen Press)
- *The Duck That Had No Luck* – Jonathan Long (Red Fox).

Cumulative tales

These often include a series of events or the introduction of characters at regular intervals as the story progresses. These tales are useful for teaching about beginnings, middles and ends, as in the 'Three seeds of a story' activity (see page 10). The end of the narrative sometimes has an explosive nature, as in 'The Enormous Turnip'. Others in this category include:

- **'Chicken Licken'** (a traditional tale)
- *Tell Us a Story* – Allan Ahlberg (Walker Books)
- **'There Was an Old Woman Who Swallowed a Fly'** (a nursery rhyme)
- **'The Enormous Turnip'** (a traditional tale)
- *The Fish Who Could Wish* – John Bush (Oxford University Press).

Circular tales

The starting point in these tales is revisited at the end, forming a kind of home and away structure. Such tales can be retold with the aid of story bags (see page 14) or through the use of story boxes (see page 24). In addition, the activity 'Stories in sound' (see page 16) can be employed with most journey tales. Stories like this include:

- *Five Little Fiends* – Sarah Dyer (Bloomsbury Children's Books)
- *Scritch Scratch* – Miriam Moss (Orchard Books)
- *Willy the Wimp* – Anthony Browne (Walker Books)
- *The House Cat* – Helen Cooper (Scholastic)
- **'The Big Wide-mouthed Toad-frog'** (page 88)
- **'Sun Frog and Moon Frog'** (page 92).

Exploring stories actively, for example collaboratively recreating Michael Rosen's famous tale, *We're Going on a Bear Hunt* (Walker Books), is the key to helping children engage with story structure in the early years and making explicit links between reading and writing in the process.

The activities in this chapter offer various ways in to active exploration of stories, and involve the children in drawing, writing or recording the story in some form.

Three seeds of a story

This activity suits well-structured stories and enables children to divide up simple tales into an opening section, a middle section and a closing section. By drawing events from the different sections of a story on to three large seeds made out of paper, children can begin to appreciate the overall structure. The use of seeds in this form is an excellent way of enabling children to retell a story in three parts. Through 'watering' the seeds with their words, the story can come to life and the fictional plant can blossom. Once children are acquainted with this activity, it can also be used for story planning, helping them to structure their own stories.

Literature links

The overtly structured retelling of traditional tales often seen in picture books are useful for this activity, for example: *What Made Tiddalik Laugh* (Puffin), *How Night Came* (Puffin), *How Rabbit Stole the Fire* (Puffin) and *How the Birds Changed Their Feathers* (Blackie Children's Books), all by Joanna Troughton. The traditional tales in this book would also work well, particularly 'Wee Meg Barnileg' (page 86), 'The Big Wide-mouthed Toad-frog' (page 88) and 'How the Tides Came to Ebb and Flow' (page 94). Other titles, for example *Boris the Brainiest Baby* and *Ruby the Rudest Girl* by Laurence Anholt (Orchard Books), would also work particularly well with more experienced readers.

What to do

❶ Cut out three large 'story seeds' from sugar paper – two small ones that can represent the beginning and the end of the tale and a much larger one for the middle – where the majority of the narrative action will take place. Also cut out a large paper flowerpot, big enough for the seeds to fit 'inside', and one small flowerpot for each child.

❷ Read your chosen story to the whole class and show the children your large flowerpot, explaining that in order for the story plant to grow, the seeds of the story need to be planted and watered with the children's words.

❸ Show the children your three blank paper seeds and discuss why they are different sizes and which part of the story they might represent. Retell the beginning of the tale and agree with the children which events you might draw in the first small seed to indicate the important opening event(s). For example, for 'Wee Meg

Barnileg' you could draw some food to reflect her fussy food habits, an item of clothing to reflect the dirty clothes she leaves for her mother to pick up and clean, and a picture of her shouting to reflect her bad behaviour.

④ Ask the class to identify the middle event(s) in the tale. Discuss these events and draw some of them on the larger middle seed, modelling the activity for the children. For example, in 'Wee Meg Barnileg' there are three tasks she has to undertake to make amends, namely clearing up the food, washing her clothes and removing the weeds which represent the unkind words she has shouted.

⑤ Ask the class, through paired discussion, to identify the final events at the end of the tale. Draw simple pictures to represent these on the small seed you are using for the ending.

⑥ The children can now make their own beginning, middle and end seeds, drawing one event on each seed which fits into one section of the story.

⑦ Organise the children into groups of three, so that they can take it in turns to plant a different seed (one beginning, middle and ending seed) in a flowerpot and retell the story in these small groups. Explain that in order to retell the story, they will need to water the seeds with their words so the story flower can grow.

Moving on

● Invite the children to select one seed and write this part of the story. A display of their work could then be assembled, to show the story in the three different sections. Ask the children to help you to arrange the separate pieces of writing in the correct order to construct the story.

● Let the children take their paper seeds home so they can share their stories with parents/carers or siblings. In this context no book is needed, and if the person at home does not know the story, so much the better.

● Later, encourage the children to use this activity to plan their own stories, drawing pictures on story seeds to use as notes for their story.

Story hands

This activity helps to develop children's awareness that stories are patterned. It introduces them to a simple structure of a beginning, middle and end, but places more emphasis on events (in these cases, a trio of events) in the middle of the story. The structure of the story is reflected in the shape of their hands. Through using simple pictures drawn in a hand shape, children can retell the tale and even use the structure to design new tales, based upon three narrative events in the middle. With experience of telling, listening, reading and writing stories, the hand frame will not be necessary. The principle of sequential narrative events, bound by an opening and a resolution or closure, will become internalised.

Literature links

Traditional tales are most suitable for this activity as they are clearly patterned. Many folk and fairy tales make use of the number three, such as three characters engaging in a significant narrative action, or events repeated three times. Such stories include 'The Three Billy Goats Gruff', 'The Three Wishes', 'The Three Little Pigs' and 'Goldilocks and the Three Bears'. You will need high-quality examples of these tales retold and/or illustrated in an engaging way, for example *Goldilocks and the Three Bears* retold by Jan Brett (Putnam Publishing Group), 'Father Bear and the Naughty Bear Cubs' in *How to Count Crocodiles* retold by Margaret Mayo (Orion Children's Books) and 'The Three Silver Balls' in *The Sea-Baby and Other Magical Stories to Read Aloud* compiled by Susan Dickinson (Collins).

What to do

❶ Read a traditional tale such as 'Goldilocks and the Three Bears', which the children are familiar with. As you tell it, encourage their active involvement, particularly in the three key actions in the middle of the tale. In 'Goldilocks' these could involve miming her trio of actions – tasting the porridge, trying out the chairs and sleeping in Baby Bear's bed.

❷ Explain to the children that as humans we all have 'story hands' which we can use to remember stories and to retell them. Discuss with them some ideas about how stories might be hidden or reflected in their hands. There is no right answer here, this is a chance for some lateral thinking and you should praise all suggestions.

❸ Demonstrate one such use by drawing around your hand on the board and explaining you are going to try to capture the story of 'Goldilocks' on the outline drawing of your hand.

④ Ask the children to discuss, in pairs, possible visuals for the beginning of the story. Agree on one simple picture and draw it in on the thumb of your story hand. Through modelling this process, the children will begin to understand it and be able to use it themselves.

© Chris Kelly

⑤ Together, revisit Goldilocks's three sets of actions in the middle of the story. From the children's ideas, draw a simple picture of each of these in the middle three fingers, for example a porridge pot, a chair and a bed.

⑥ Invite the children to suggest what visual needs to be drawn in the last or little finger to indicate the end of the tale. Draw this in; it could be, for example, Goldilocks running home.

⑦ Ask the children to retell the tale, working in small groups and using the class hand as a prompt to recall the structure of the events.

⑧ Then retell another tale, one the children know and can join in with actively, such as 'The Three Billy Goats Gruff'. Identify three physical actions for the trio of events in this tale to help imprint these in the minds of the children.

⑨ Invite pairs or individuals to draw around their hands and depict in simple visuals the events at the beginning, middle and end of the story.

⑩ Use these story hands to retell the tale. This could be in done in groups of four –

one child opens and closes the story, the three others each retell a significant middle event.

⑪ Individually, the children could choose one part of the story they wish to retell and compose a written paragraph which reflects the visuals.

Moving on

● Invite the children to write key words in each finger instead of, or as well as, drawing pictures.

● Model drawing a bracelet around the wrist of your original story hand. This encircles the whole story and can represent the theme of the narrative. Key words from the story can then be written in the bracelet or pictures drawn to show the theme.

● When the children are more experienced at using story hands to capture the structure of a known tale, they could go on to plan their own stories, using the hand as a planning tool for the structure.

Story bags

There are two key purposes of this activity. The first is to provide children with an opportunity to revisit favourite stories, particularly those with strong narrative structures, and to consolidate their repertoire. This will remind them of the range of stories they can lean on as writers. The second purpose is to support the children in a playful activity as they develop their understanding of the main elements that make up a story. By using simple artefacts, clearly representative of different components of a story, children will have prompts for their retelling of it. This will help them in planning oral, drawn and written stories by giving them the initial support of a concrete experience on which to base future, more abstract writing activities.

Literature links

For this activity children need access to a range of high-quality picture fiction with which they are familiar. The most appropriate books are those that have very simple themes and which can be easily represented in story bags, for example: *Dear Greenpeace* by Simon James, *Little Lumpty* by Miko Imai, *Owl Babies* by Martin Waddell (all published by Walker Books) or *Rover* by Michael Rosen (Bloomsbury Children's Books). The books to be used for this activity could be collected together in a box or basket so that the children can easily identify them. Some traditional tales, such as those given in this book (pages 86–96), could also be used for this purpose as they have clear structures and patterns which children should find easy to remember and replicate.

What to do

1. Use brightly coloured or decorative cloth bags that can be easily recognised as 'story bags'. Support staff and parents/carers could be asked to make a collection of these or they can be purchased from some booksellers.

2. First, model the activity, with the children participating in the joint composition of the story. With the story of *Owl Babies* in mind, for example, present the bag, already containing finger puppets of owls, feathers, leaves and twigs, and pull out the owls. It would help to capture the children's imagination if this could be achieved with a sense of mystery and wonder,

deliberating on what story could possibly feature a family of owls. Then produce the feathers, leaves and twigs, encouraging the children to describe the owls' home, depicted on the first page of the book, and to begin the retelling of the story. Encourage progression of the story, by taking from the bag a big branch, a small branch and an old bit of ivy. And finally, a picture or finger puppet representing the swooping mother owl, as she returns at the end of the story, can be shown.

❸ A number of bags could be collected, each containing a group of objects representing a pre-selected range of stories. Choose items that can be clearly identified with different stages of the story. For example, in *Dear Greenpeace* the first item could be a toy whale, the second some salt, the third a picture of blue water, the next cornflakes and breadcrumbs (or a picture of these) and the last a seaside picture and a sandwich.

❹ In a whole-class session, invite a child to 'blindly' select a bag. A second child could then pull out an item, and then a third and so on until the bag is empty. Ask the children to guess the story to which the items belong.

❺ The children should then, with their combined knowledge of the story, discuss the order in which these objects or story prompts appear. Scribe their suggestions on the board.

❻ Invite individual children to retell to the class each section of the story, with digressions, inventions or embellishments encouraged!

❼ On completion, ask another child to identify from the box/basket/book area the book of the told story. Read the original version of the story to satisfy the children that their order of events matched that of the original author.

Moving on

● Use the story bags during quiet reading time or as an independent activity during the Literacy Hour when the children could work in pairs. Ask them to take turns to select from the bag and place the items in order on the table in preparation for a retelling of the story.

● Ask the children to illustrate their story items, taken from a story bag, in the form of storyboards. Encourage them to begin to subtitle the images with words or phrases that represent the themes and events of the tale.

© Chris Kelly

Stories in sound

The purpose of this activity is to use sound to recreate a well-known story. As a whole class or large group, the children create a physical storyboard and evoke the sounds explicitly given and implicitly suggested in a story. Their sound collage is used to accompany an oral retelling or re-reading of the tale. This enlivens the narrative and helps the children dwell inside the tale's structure, feeling its tunes and rhythms and gaining an insight into a character's emotional journey. This activity also usefully highlights major episodes in a plot and helps children to understand time structure and sequential relationships in stories. The significant events in the tale are captured in the physical storyboard (which is in effect a series of freeze-frames) and a sound journey of the tale is created.

What to do

❶ Select a story from those mentioned below that is well known to the children and re-read it to them.

❷ Explain to the children that together you are going to make a series of freeze-frames or still pictures, to represent the story, by miming part of the action of the story and then freezing in this position. This will show the story structure – the journey that the main character took through the narrative.

❸ Create a series of whole-class freeze-frames to show the main character's journey, or give each group a different part of the story to depict. For example, for *Where the Wild*

WHERE THE WILD THINGS ARE

STORY AND PICTURES BY MAURICE SENDAK

Literature links

This activity works most evocatively with 'journey tales' as these are often clearly episodic in character. Some, for example *Where the Wild Things Are* by Maurice Sendak (Red Fox) and *This Is the Bear* by Sarah Hayes (Walker Books) return to the same starting point, with Max returning to his home and the bear being found by its owner. Others reach a climax before they are resolved, for example *What Made Tiddalik Laugh* by Joanna Troughton (Puffin) in which the platypus saves the day and

Tiddalik returns all the waters of the world to the Earth. Other stories that work well with this activity include: *The Rainbow Fish* by Marcus Pfister (North–South Books), *Willy the Wimp* by Anthony Browne (Walker Books), *Can't You Sleep, Little Bear?* by Martin Waddell (Walker Books) and *Not Now, Bernard* by David McKee (Red Fox). Most of these stories show the main character's response to their journey or the outcome of the journey.

Things Are, seven class freeze-frames could be made, covering:

1 the night Max made mischief
2 his travel on board his boat
3 his meeting with the Wild Things
4 his time as king (sending the Wild Things to bed without any supper)
5 his loneliness and desire to go home
6 his sailing home
7 his arrival back in his bedroom (to find his supper still hot!).

④ Focus on one of the freeze-frames, and ask the children to think of the sounds which might be heard at that moment in the text. For example, when Max travels on the boat perhaps he can hear the sea, seagulls, the noises of the Wild Things in the distance, the blow of a ship's horn, dolphins calling to one another.

⑤ Try not to shape this creative activity too closely. As the children are sitting still in the boat as Max, suggest they make their noises together to create a sound collage (using voice and body percussion). Request silence with a tambour.

⑥ Move around the class, touching children on the shoulder and asking them to make their sound individually. Can the rest of the children guess what the sound is? If necessary, ask the child who has been touched on the shoulder to explain.

⑦ Create each freeze-frame in sequence, giving all the children a chance to contribute a sound to the story.

⑧ Together create the story in sound, with you reading the tale and the children making the noises in sequence (without being in their freeze-frames).

⑨ Select one or two parts and recreate those freeze-frames, asking the children to voice the words that could be heard at that moment. What might Max be saying or thinking when he meets the wild creatures for the first time? What might they be asking him?

⑩ Ask different children to draw Max's face and write speech or thought bubbles at a chosen moment in the text. Arrange these speech bubbles in order on a large poster that reflects the seven freeze-frames. In this way you will have created, evoked and reflected upon the character's journey, and will have identified and experienced the key episodes in the tale.

© Eyewire

Moving on

● The children's pictures and speech/thought bubbles can be made into an instant story book.

● Consider sharing the story in sound, with its accompanying freeze-frames, in an assembly or with another class.

● In music or literacy, the children could use percussion instruments to create scary stories in sound, stories with a sudden surprise, and so on.

The story cauldron

This activity highlights the ingredients of a good story (beginning, setting, characters, problems, resolution) and teaches children how to put together a clear structure in a story. Through shared writing, it gives them the knowledge of how to plan for story narratives in a way that will enable them to go through the process independently. When telling the children your story you may want to get up and move around to keep them interested, and invite them to help you out from time to time by offering you their ideas (*And what do you think*

Literature links

Books that have very clear structures and a good story to tell would be appropriate for this activity, such as *Mr Tick the Teacher* by Allan Ahlberg (Puffin). *West Indian Folk-tales* retold by Philip Sherlock (Oxford University Press) can also be used to introduce children to stories from another culture. These stories have a rich history woven into their narrative. The tales in *Aesop's Funky Fables* by Vivian French (Puffin) are a fun way to introduce young children to classic fables. *Buffy: An Adventure Story* by Bob Graham (Walker Books) is a modern tale with a 'blues' feel to it.

happened next?). **You can also involve the children by asking individuals to stand up and be different characters in the story.**

What to do

❶ Make a magic cauldron; it can be two-dimensional, using a large piece of card cut into the shape of a cauldron, or you may even want to use a three-dimensional one – a simply adapted magic story saucepan is sure to work! Create the ingredients of a special story by writing *beginning, setting, main characters, problems* and *resolution* on story cards, each element of the story on a separate card. You may want to use different coloured cards so that you can identify them easily.

❷ Place your story cards in the cauldron and use them to retell a story. This may be a traditional story you know, one from this book, such as 'Wee Meg Barnileg' (page

86), or a familiar story from the classroom collection.

③ Tell the story, giving it plenty of impact by stirring the cauldron each time you pull out a card, as if the cauldron contained a potent, magical storytelling mixture. Have some fun at this stage: pointing to the children, throw a smile and some laughter into the cauldron. Or perhaps give it a serious look or a happy face, pretending to take the expression from the children you point to. Ask the children to stir the cauldron with you, either inviting individual children to come and do it, or asking everyone to do a stirring movement with their hands.

④ Attach the cards to a flipchart to retell another story with the children, but this time use the cards as a planning frame for a shared writing session. Write a short paragraph for each card on the flipchart. These paragraphs can then form the basis of a rich retelling as 'flesh' is slowly added to the bare bones of the tale. You may wish to concentrate on a particular part of the story, the introduction or resolution for example, so the writing might only be done at this point in the retelling – it's up to you.

Moving on

● Use the cards for children to work in pairs, planning a retelling of a story they know well. The cards, as in the shared writing activity, will guide the children in structuring their retelling of the tale. They will remember your storytelling and this will assist them in gaining motivation and ideas. The children should know plenty of stories, but you may need to remind them of the detail by brainstorming some, thus providing a menu for them to draw upon.

● Many stories across a variety of genres have similar structures. If you are focusing on fantasy stories, for example, let the children use the cards as a basis for their own stories.

Beginning

A long long time ago there lived a tiny little girl called Wee Meg Barnileg. There has never been a child who had been more spoiled than her. She was fussy about every little thing that was offered to her – food, clothes and gifts – and she was always rude about other people that she came across.

When her mother offered her tasty morsels of food she would say: "Oh, I don't want that, I don't like that."

When her granny bought her lovely clothes she would say: "Oh, I won't wear that, I don't like that."

And she would laugh at other people's misfortunes: "Oh, look Mummy," she would say cruelly, "that girl's got no shoes. Ha ha, hee hee."

Wee Meg Barnileg was also cruel to animals. She liked to poke the poor farmer's dog who was kept chained up in all weathers and if he ever snapped at her for being unkind, she would run crying and hollering to her mother.

Her family fussed over her all the time, but Wee Meg Barnileg gave them no thanks, only shouting ungratefully at them and screaming about how they didn't care for her.

Setting

The Barnilegs lived in a tiny village in the middle of the countryside. A river wound its way around the little smoking houses and parish church that made up the community of farmers and farm labourers who had lived and worked in the same place for many a year. The wind would blow through the trees that lined the single dirt road that led in and out of the village. In a small stone cottage that stood on the outskirts of the village lived a tiny lass with the name of Wee Meg Barnileg.

Stepping stones to cross the river

End

Beginning

This activity invites children to engage in storytelling that is supported by a frame of 'stepping stones'. The frame reflects the structure of the story narrative, thereby enabling children to plan a retelling based on the structure they have followed. The beauty of this activity is that the children can use the stepping stones structure to plan their own stories. Physical movement in activities at school helps children to remember the concepts that are being taught. Asking the children to stand on the stepping stones and leap to the next one as each section of the story is told will reinforce learning. It also helps transform a literacy lesson of sitting still into an active and fun way to learn.

What to do

① Retell a story that the children will enjoy and engage with. You may wish to use one of the stories retold in this book – 'The Big Wide-mouthed Toad-frog' is great and always enjoyed by children of this

Literature links

Re-workings of traditional stories and fables are particularly suitable for this activity. Children react with glee to *There's a Wolf in My Pudding* by David Henry Wilson (Macmillan) as the tales proceed in unexpected directions. *Way Out West With a Baby* by Mike Brownlow (Ragged Bears) is written as a ballad, drawing on the traditions of the Western, and is especially appealing to children in this age group. *Squids Will Be Squids* by Jon Scieszka (Puffin) plays deliciously with old tales whilst keeping strong structures and *The Young Oxford Book of Folk Tales* by Kevin Crossley-Holland provides good, clear retellings.

particular age. Remember to make the story come alive by retelling it in an animated way. Encourage the children to predict what might happen next by asking questions as you go, and allow children to make connections between the events and characters in the stories and their own lives.

© Chris Kelly

❷ Let the children comment on what strikes them about the tale. They may make links with what the characters are doing by comparing the characters' behaviour with their own lives. You can also use places described in the story to encourage the children to remember where they have visited, and they should be given the opportunity to discuss these. Of course, you will have to make a professional decision about when to move on!

❸ Draw on the board a series of five stones that cross a river. These will be the different sections of the story that you have told. The river banks could be used to indicate the beginning and the end of the story.

❹ Ask the children to tell you what happened of significance at the start of the story. Then ask for three events that occurred during the story and, finally, how the story ended. Write key words or draw depictions of the key events on the individual stones.

❺ Invite the children to work in pairs, using a sheet with the stones drawn on it to illustrate and write their way across the river, until they get to the end of the story. Wherever you can, you should encourage talk in the classroom, and asking the children to work in pairs on a story will

create opportunities for this shared kind of learning.

❻ Ask chosen groups to retell the story using their stones to help them. Listen to the vocabulary they are using. Do you see the children copying the way in which you told the story earlier on?

Moving on

● The stones are an excellent way to plan a story. Give the children a small sheet of paper with stones drawn on. They can then rough out the story using the stones to guide them.

● Draw and cut out large stones from card or fabric to place on the floor. Ask a child to jump from stone to stone as the story is told and the structure of the story moves on. Make sure that the material you are using for the stones is non-slip!

● Sets of children could freeze-frame the events that happen on each stone. Give each group one stone and ask the children to create a frozen representation. As the children retell the story and reach the different stepping stones, those on the relevant stone form their freeze-frame.

Story journey scrolls

The purpose of this activity is to help children develop their understanding of the sequence of events in a story and the language used to describe time passing. It also allows children to join with others in their group to construct and retell stories together. Collecting and using books that contain a clear sense of a journey will greatly aid younger children's learning. By retelling the stories, initially in a highly supported way as a whole class with the teacher modelling key vocabulary, the children can be encouraged to use language that indicates sequence in the story journey. Physically mapping the journey of the story on a roll of paper in this activity will help young children to create concrete images which will later develop into the more abstract activity of writing. As they become more experienced in this kind of story representation, they could use role-play, dolls, puppets and small-world apparatus to provide the physical supports for their journey reconstructions.

Literature links

Stories that contain journeys, such as *Mr Gumpy's Motor Car* and *Mr Gumpy's Outing* by John Burningham (Red Fox), *We're Going on a Bear Hunt* by Michael Rosen (Walker Books) or *Can't You Sleep Little Bear?* by Martin Waddell (Walker Books), would be useful for this activity as the action is sequential through the length of the journey in the tale. A short and simple story to use to begin with, and to model this kind of activity to the children would be *Where's My Teddy?* by Jez Alborough (Walker Books). This would help the children to be clear in their retelling. Traditional tales also often contain a journey element, for example 'Little Red Riding Hood' or 'The Big Wide-mouthed Toad-frog' (see page 88).

What to do

1 This activity will work well with the whole class in a large space, for example the hall, or with small groups on the carpet area.

2 Read or retell one of the suggested stories to the group, encouraging the children to join in with patterned language or refrains in the story.

3 Discuss the story with the children, referring back to the pictures and the text in the book to emphasise the key points in the journey, and encourage questions and responses.

④ Unroll a long strip of paper across the floor (a roll of wallpaper, used on the reverse side to the pattern, will serve this purpose).

⑤ Using, for example, *Where's My Teddy?* by Jez Alborough, explain to the children that one child will represent Eddy and will walk by the side of the paper, along the length of the roll to its end – and, therefore, the end of the story.

⑥ At points along the journey the rest of the group should stop this child when something happens in the story. Ask the children quickly to draw a picture or write a few words or phrases that represent the particular event. For example, at the beginning of *Where's My Teddy?* Eddy can be drawn with marks to represent the trees in the woods. The second stage could be when he says 'Help!', and so on, until the end of the book and the journey, when the bear and Eddy are safe in their own beds.

⑦ Initially the drawing and/or writing could be carried out by you, in order to model appropriate representative images or words. A sense of excitement could be created by generating questions to engage the children. Stopping the child on the journey to ask how he or she feels at each stage would also help to create an atmosphere.

⑧ It should be emphasised that this is not an activity in which careful drawings or correct spellings are required, but rather a quick representation to mark each stage of the journey.

⑨ It would be helpful to model appropriate vocabulary (such as, *First…, and then…, suddenly…, until…, soon…*), so that the children gather a sense of a sequence of events occurring and time passing on the journey towards a final outcome.

⑩ The paper could then be rolled into a scroll and unravelled stage by stage, to emphasise the journey, as the class joins in a retelling of the story.

Moving on

● During literacy activity times, the children could be invited in pairs to embellish the story journey scroll with further illustrations and annotations.

● Ask pairs of children to work together, using the scroll, to retell the story in a literacy activity time.

● Smaller blank story scrolls could be made available in the writing corner for children to create story journeys or recreate those already known to them.

● Props, such as hats, coats, scarves, boots, cloaks, bags, sacks, rucksacks and picnic baskets, could be made available in the role-play area to prompt children to recreate journeys from stories in their play.

© Chris Kelly

Story boxes

This activity makes use of familiar tales, as suggested in Helen Bromley's work on story boxes (*Primary English Magazine* January/February 1999). It is designed to provide young children with an opportunity to construct their own stories or reconstruct familiar tales, using a collection of small objects to prompt their memory of events or experiences. It will support the children as they develop a grasp of narrative structures. During this activity children improve their ability to structure their stories, often by using as a model a tale they know well and by using conventional story-book language at the beginning and end (such as, *Once upon a time...* or, *First there was a...* and *They all lived happily ever after...* or, *They all went home to bed*). Initially, the children may need the support of an adult to guide them or to ask leading questions, but they will soon become independent in this activity.

Literature links

Familiar stories that would be used successfully in this activity include *Owl Babies* by Martin Waddell, *Where's My Teddy?* by Jez Alborough, *This is the Bear* by Sarah Hayes, *Little Lumpty* by Miko Imai (all Walker Books) or indeed any familiar traditional tale or nursery rhyme. However, if topics such as 'The seaside' or Christmas have been explored in the classroom, then it may be appropriate to use texts based on one of these rather than a more general literature model.

What to do

❶ Construct a simple story box from a shoebox: cut down the corners of one long side so that it flaps down to extend the surface. Choose items for the box that are relevant to your chosen story, but keep them minimal so that children concentrate on reconstructing the story rather than focusing on the objects. The resources in the story box are only intended to act as props to support the construction or the retelling of the story.

❷ This activity is best suited to children working in very small groups, pairs or individually. Read your chosen story to the children. Then encourage a discussion by asking questions and allowing the children to respond with their thoughts and ideas.

❸ Show the children the story box, explaining what it contains. Invite the children to explore the box and its resources, giving them an opportunity to talk and play independently.

❹ Initially, you may want to remind the children, as they are playing, of the main themes, the journey or the key events of the story. You may also want to question them, for example, if you are using *Little Lumpty* as the text: *What's going to happen next? Is he going to fall this time? How do you think he will get down from the wall?* It will be helpful to model 'doing the voices' of the characters, although some children will do this naturally.

❺ Once the children are familiar with the relationship between the props and the story, provide a pair of children with the props and encourage them to use them for a retelling.

6 If you have chosen to base the story box on a specific topic or theme rather than the narrative of a story book, discuss the topic with the children. For example, talk about what you might find at the seaside and what kind of stories might take place there. Or, you might want to ask the children to recall in pairs what happens in the story of the nativity or to invent a new story in a Christmas setting. This could be a story about an angel, a shepherd or a reindeer. At this stage, you may want to make links with books the children know well that also reflect the theme or tell the story.

7 Give the children relevant props in the story box to help them to visualise the story they are creating. For example, in the Nativity, this may be straw, a small baby doll or figurine, and some model farm animals.

8 Talk about how the story might begin in order to help the children make a start. You may want to provide the children with choices of other resources to enhance their story boxes and to extend their stories.

9 Allow the children time to construct their stories in a free-flow way, without feeling constrained by any predetermined structures or intended outcomes.

10 Give children the opportunity to share their stories with others in their group.

CORNWALL COLLEGE
LEARNING CENTRE

Moving on

● A collection of story boxes could be made available to the children to use in pairs during a Literacy Hour or a quiet reading time.

● It will be beneficial to the children and to their development as storytellers if the activity is taped or scribed by an adult and subsequently shared with others. This written or taped version of the story should be stored with the story box and the book, if used, so that it is available as an additional resource in the future.

● Books with similar themes could be grouped with a story box containing appropriate resources. This will help the children to see the connection between texts and to classify according to theme. It will also provide them with a repertoire from which they can select to mix and match in their story box retelling.

Change the ending

The aim of this activity is to enable children to compose alternative endings to stories. By considering and choosing from three different types of conclusion (funny, surprising or sad), children are able to take control of the story, allowing them to feel the power that a writer can have when creating an ending. The activity also emphasises how stories finish within the structure of a whole narrative. With the teacher's guidance, the children are encouraged to discuss their ideas with their partners and with the whole class. The children will enjoy putting their mark on the story and the activity should result in rich generative talk and good pieces of writing.

What to do

❶ Read your chosen story to the children in full.

❷ Go through the story, discussing it in some detail from start to finish. Stop at various points in the tale to question and explain the events or talk about the characters.

❸ You may wish the children to do a short role-play activity, taking on the voice and character of some of the protagonists in the story. This kind of interaction will help to keep the children's attention and will encourage them to attempt these reading techniques on their own.

Literature links

Well-illustrated picture books are ideal for this activity. The following stories are all by significant children's authors. Each has an unusual conclusion, and all of them could have been written to end quite differently. Some stories have endings that the children will not want altered, but they may enjoy the opportunity to experiment with others. *The Heron and the Crane* by John Yeoman and Quentin Blake (Puffin) really makes the reader frustrated for the right ending. *John Brown, Rose and the Midnight Cat* by Jenny Wagner (Puffin) is a stunning picture book that has simplicity and depth, and has a perfect conclusion in the sense that it is mysterious, but the children will be able to think of alternatives. *Grunter: The Story of a Pig With Attitude* by Mike Jolley (Templar) is a very funny tale with an ethical discussion waiting to happen. *Mrs Vole the Vet* by Allan Ahlberg (Puffin) has Mrs Vole's children trying to find her a boyfriend. Does Mrs Vole make the right choice? Alternatively, you could experiment with a familiar and well-loved story, such as *Owl Babies* by Martin Waddell (Walker Books), or a traditional tale, such as 'Jack and the Beanstalk'. From this book you could use 'The Wrestling Animals' and 'The Big Wide-mouthed Toad-frog' (pages 90 and 88).

④ Tell the children that, as a class, you are going to make up different endings for the story. Take suggestions from the children on how you might change it, for example a sad ending, a surprising ending or a funny ending.

⑤ Depending on the age and the ability of the children, you may need to model some ideas to help the children understand what you would like them to do. For example, if you are looking at 'The Big Wide-mouthed Toad-frog', you might want to share the surprise ending in the box below with them.

⑥ Give the children a little more time, if necessary, to come up with some other ideas for surprise endings on their own.

⑦ Share some examples of the children's surprise endings. Were they surprising? Did the surprise also have an additional effect, for example, what it comical or frightening?

⑧ Now ask the children to work in pairs to make up their own *sad* ending for the story. Encourage the children to listen carefully to their partners and to develop their ideas together.

⑨ Ask the various pairs to tell you and the rest of the group their alternative conclusion for the story. Again, discuss the effects of these, and together as a class decide which one you like most. Ask the children to explain their reasons for thinking this sad ending is the best.

Surprising ending

Now the last creature the Big Wide-mouthed Toad-frog met on his way looked like a long green log, with white roots glinting in the sunshine. "Hello! Hello! Hell..." said Big Wide-mouthed Toad-frog.

"Well, heh, heh, heh, I'm an alligator and I just love to eat Big Wide-mouthed Toad-frogs" snarled the alligator after swallowing the frog whole and looking around him with a glint in his eye.

If you ever come across that mean green alligator, if you listen really hard, you might just hear a tiny little voice from way down in the depths of that alligator's stomach saying: "Hello! Hello! Hello! What are you and what do you like to eat?"

The alligator came to call it indigestion.

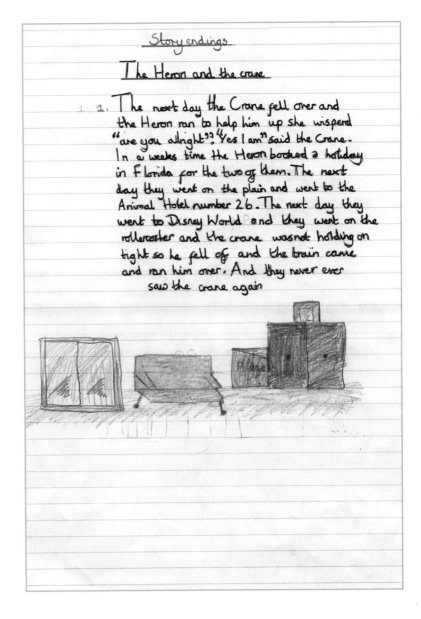

⑩ Ask the children if they consider any of these surprise or sad endings to be better than the original ending to the story. Encourage them to tell you why (or why not).

⑪ You may wish to construct a more complete text for the new sad ending, with you scribing the children's ideas on to the board. As you write, think aloud, make changes and generally model the drafting process. This is a great opportunity to teach at text, sentence and word level. The content of your talk here will often depend on the point in the writing process the text has reached. If it's a first draft then composition and the meaning of the piece will be highlighted. There will be less emphasis here on the transcription, but this would be more important if the writing had reached the proof-reading stage. Ponder over spellings and discuss the strategies writers can use to find the correct spellings – asking a friend, looking in the dictionary, sounding the words out, looking around the classroom for the spelling, or leaving a gap to go back to it later. Keep reading the passage back, looking for ways to improve the phrasing – a different word, punctuation to help the reader and so on.

⑫ Ask the children, in pairs, to draft and illustrate a funny ending to the story, experimenting on whiteboards or paper. As the children are writing, ask for examples so ideas can be shared and built upon during the session rather than at the end, when it's too late!

Moving on

● Invite the children to present their work in a display that incorporates their own drawings and illustrations from the books you have used. Children will need a clear purpose and an audience for their writing and illustrations, and the display provides both. Remember to inform them before they start writing!

● Make the display interactive, asking the viewers which ending they prefer. By providing a pad of sticky labels children can be invited to write their answers and views and stick them around the display.

● Re-read the story to the class and naturally weave in the ending that a pair of children has written. By linking the published tale with the endings written by the children, there will almost be a seamless link – this is a real thrill for the young writers.

Chapter Two

Characterisation

p31 Adopting roles

p32 Hot-seating

p34 Thought-tracking

p36 Will you be my friend?

p38 I need a home

p40 Characters in the family

p42 Character ladders

p44 Understanding Mister Wolf

p46 Character pockets

p48 Shaking out characters

Characters have a powerful and determining role in the story. The reader identifies with the story through its characters and often stories are referred to by a character's name. The main character's name may indeed be part of the title.

Certain kinds of characters are often used to create certain kinds of stories. Ogres, giants, witches and goblins make frightening children's books, while rabbits, baby owls and moles are generally found in gentler tales. Each kind of character will evoke different feelings in readers.

The activities in this chapter are designed to help children develop their understanding of the function of characters in stories. A range of wonderful tales are suggested for use, and the children are encouraged to discuss their feelings about the actions and behaviours of the characters in these stories.

All the best writers in history were great readers and, by introducing children to a variety of characters, their potential to be good writers themselves will be greatly increased.

In school, teachers often encourage exploration of characters on a personal level. This will mean 'getting to know' the characters, thinking of them as real people and sharing their experiences in an imaginary way. Characters in a story can often be used as a way to judge our own behaviour in the real world. The actions that story-book characters take may even shape the decisions we choose to make in later life.

Critical debate about a fictional character's thoughts and deeds calls for a range of higher-order reading skills that challenge children at important intellectual levels. Trying to understand a character's actions needs an examination of cause – both physical and emotional – and requires the capacity to empathise and connect with a character's feelings and predicaments. Children aged between five and seven are willing to talk about books in this way. Their ability to do so should not be underestimated – they will have much to say on these matters. Many of the activities in this chapter, such as 'Adopting roles' or 'Will you be my friend?' have a playful spirit that the children will understand and thoroughly enjoy.

In the National Literacy Strategy teachers are asked to encourage children to identify and discuss characters, and activities, like role-play, are suggested to reinforce learning. This chapter provides many ideas to help teachers to successfully organise a rich variety of learning experiences.

The exploration of character will nearly always begin with children talking about the heroes and heroines of stories with which they are familiar. The Literacy Hour and its components should allow teachers time to immerse the class in a range of texts full of rich characters. Role-play and drama provide opportunities to learn about the characters from 'inside' the stories during imaginative engagement with scenes that make up the narrative. Shared reading will allow teachers to discuss and highlight how writers create believable and realistic people in their stories. Shared writing gives opportunities to model the construction of texts with strong characterisation. Descriptions of appearance, personality and behaviour can be generated together, to teach the fundamentals of effective character writing.

Fortunately, there are stacks of books written for children that have wonderful characters in them. Here are some examples that we have used in the activities in this chapter:

- *Owl Babies* – Martin Waddell (Walker Books)
- *Rover* – Michael Rosen (Bloomsbury Children's Books)
- *Where's My Teddy?* – Jez Alborough (Walker Books)
- *Clarice Bean, That's Me!* – Lauren Child (Orchard Books)
- *Football Crazy* – Colin McNaughton (Mammoth)
  - *This Is the Bear and the Scary Night* – Sarah Hayes (Walker Books)
    - *The Time It Took Tom* – Nick Sharratt and Stephen Tucker (Scholastic).

Adopting roles

The purpose of this activity is to help children develop empathy for characters in books by adopting their perspective. By taking on a particular role, children begin to develop insight into a character's traits, motives and behaviour. Possible conversations can be created and the character's reactions can be improvised. This is a useful shared reading activity, focusing on character and comprehension. It can also lead to shared or independent writing in role, such as a letter to another character or a diary entry.

Literature links

Most books involve characters encountering difficulties and these make substantial material for role-play. In *The Time It Took Tom* by Nick Sharratt and Stephen Tucker (Scholastic), Mum arrives to find Tom has painted the entire living room (and the cat) bright red. Whatever does she say? How does he explain himself? The following texts and many others could also be used: *Willa and Old Miss Annie* by Berlie Doherty (Walker Books), *Angry Arthur* by Hiawyn Oram (Red Fox), *The Train Ride* by June Crebbin (Walker Books), *My Friend Bear* by Jez Alborough (Walker Books) and *Mrs Cockle's Cat* by Philippa Pearce (Puffin).

What to do

1. Choose a story with two significant characters and the potential for a role-play activity. Read a passage from the story prior to the selected moment. A good moment would be one involving a difference of opinion. In *The Time It Took Tom*, for example, use the scene when Mum arrives and finds that Tom has painted the sitting room red!

2. Invite the children to work in pairs and adopt the role of a character. Ponder aloud some possibilities for what the characters might say to each other. If using *The Time It Took Tom*, invite the children to suggest what their own mothers might say!

3. Narrate the previous part of the story again and, joining a partner yourself, ask the pairs to role-play the conversation that Mum and Tom might have had.

4. Alternatively, you could take the role of Tom and the children the role of Mum. In this case, try to explain your actions and respond earnestly to 'Mum's' responses. Scribe some of Mum's comments in speech bubbles and possible replies from Tom.

5. Finish reading the book, stopping at a later point to role-play the same characters in a different situation.

Moving on

- Ask the children to role-play persuasive conversations, for example, in *Angry Arthur* by Hiawyn Oram, Arthur wants to stay up and watch television and tries to persuade his mum to let him.

- Following role-play, invite the children to take part in a writing activity. If you have role-played *The Time It Took Tom*, ask the children to 'be Tom' and to write an apology to his mother. Or, for *Angry Arthur*, Arthur might record a diary entry the evening that he missed his favourite Western on television.

Hot-seating

The purpose of this activity is to build up knowledge about a character through focused questioning in role, then to reflect upon this knowledge, perhaps using it in future work. This is a valuable shared reading activity, which enables simple profiles to be built describing the character's appearance, behaviour and attitudes. Two or more children as well as adults can be hot-seated together, representing one character from the text. The questioners should also adopt a clear role in relation to the character and should ask relevant questions from that point of view. The information gathered needs to be summarised or recorded in some form, so that facts and opinions about the character can be identified. The text can then be re-read to ascertain the author's words and phrases which describe this individual.

What to do

❶ Select a difficult moment in a story for a particular character and read up to that point in the text.

❷ Ask the children if they would like to know more about the character and what they are feeling at this particular moment. How do they imagine the character might be feeling? Why?

❸ Identify between one and three volunteers willing to sit on the hot-seat and go into role as the main character. Then agree the range of roles for the rest of the class as questioners. Give the children time to think of questions or to generate some background information about their character in order to ask questions. For example, in *The Rainbow Fish* they could be other fish wanting his silver scales, the

Literature links

Tension or challenge in some form is important in all stories and often raises further questions from the reader. Hot-seating is a useful activity for moments in the narrative when there is a desire to know more about a particular character. Identifying a relevant moment is important, for example, in *The Rainbow Fish* by Marcus Pfister (North–South Books), the fish has no friends because he will not share his

MARCUS PFISTER
THE RAINBOW FISH
NORTH-SOUTH BOOKS

silver scales. He goes to talk to a starfish to whom he is able to reveal his past and his fears about the present. The children, in role, can find out why the Rainbow Fish does not want to share his scales. In *The Teddy Robber* by Ian Beck (Corgi), a giant is stealing children's teddies. On meeting him the children will be able to find out the kind of giant he is and may be able to help him. In this example it is important not to have read the whole story to the class, but to stop at the moment the giant hides Tom's teddy. Other appropriate texts include the story 'How the Tides Came to Ebb and Flow' (see page 94). The great Sky Spirit To Whom All Things Belonged could be interviewed by a newspaper to find out his reasons for not granting the old woman a hut to live in.

starfish wanting to understand the situation, King Neptune wanting harmony in the ocean, or even reporters from the 'Ocean News'. If appropriate, provide whiteboards for the children to record the questions.

④ Re-read the previous part of the story and then introduce the hot-seat in a fictional manner. In effect you are trying to create the situation as real. Say, for example: *The Rainbow Fish was tired, he swam down to the bottom of the ocean and lay on the floor of the sea. Onlookers gathered around him, the word spread on the waves that the vainglorious Rainbow Fish might well give an interview. Fish came from all around until he was surrounded... Let's find out what happened...*

⑤ Prepare the children to challenge those characters on the hot-seat. First, as a model, put yourself in role as Rainbow Fish and get the Learning Support Assistant to ask you more demanding and probing questions. You are trying to avoid questions that can be answered monosyllabically, with just a *Yes* or *No*. This modelling will help the children to see which kinds of questions reveal most about the character.

⑥ After all of the volunteers have taken a turn in the hot-seat, ask the children to say what they now know about the character. Concentrate initially on his or her appearance – if you have not shared the pictures in the story book, the children are likely to have built up a picture of the character in their minds from the hot-seat alone. Record and compare their descriptions and encourage the children to give reasons for their answers, such as recalling what those in the hot-seat said in response to a question.

⑦ Focus on the other facts about the character as revealed by the hot-seat, and ask the children to recall relevant words or phrases used.

© Chris Kelly

⑧ Summarise this character profile on the flipchart, helping the children explain their views with reference to the hot-seating.

⑨ Read on in the text and ask the children to clap when the author uses any words or phrases to describe the character. Initially, this will not be easy, but with more experience this is a useful way of noticing the writer's descriptive words and comparing these with the insights gained through the hot-seating.

Moving on

● You could extend this activity into writing by making simple character profiles of the character with pictures and words. Alternatively, you could help the class write from the role they adopted, perhaps in the form of a diary, newspaper article, magazine interview or letter.

● Later on in the text, you might organise small group hot-seats and share significant new findings about the character from these.

Thought-tracking

This activity focuses on the inner voice and views of characters. It involves thinking out loud as a character in a text, and exploring feelings and thoughts at a challenging or thought-provoking moment in the story. This will encourage empathy and also extend the children's use of role language. The activity can be organised with everyone speaking a character's thoughts aloud (thought-tracking), or a chair or object can represent the character and children are invited to step forward and voice their thoughts in role. Connections to characters' emotions can be made to enable children to write parallel tales in which they experienced fear or anger themselves.

What to do

① Read your chosen book to the class, pausing at a thought-provoking moment – one which you aim to use to develop thought-tracking. For instance, if reading *This is the Bear and the Scary Night* by Sarah Hayes (Walker Books), you could stop when the bear is abandoned and left alone in the park.

② In role as the bear, ponder out loud how you feel – abandoned, forgotten and cold, especially as night falls and the moon rises, making shadows and

Literature links

In most narratives one of the key characters experiences a challenge or problem. For example, in *The Magical Bicycle* by Berlie Doherty (Picture Lions), the boy finds it hard to ride his bicycle; he is initially despondent and later elated – both moments would suit thought-tracking. In *Goldilocks and the Three Bears* by Jan Brett (Putnam Publishing Group), Baby Bear looks thoughtfully at the sleeping Goldilocks – what is he thinking? In a circle with a chair in the middle and a plaited rope hung over its back to represent Goldilocks, the children could step forward and voice their views in role as Baby Bear. In *This Is the Bear and the Scary Night* by Sarah Hayes (Walker Books), the bear is left alone in the dark park. How does he feel and what can he see in the darkness? In *A Baby for Grace* by Ian Whybrow (Kingfisher), Grace finds it hard to adjust to a new baby sister – how does she feel? In *Fisherwitch* by Susan Gates (Scholastic), the boy is terrified of the fictional Fisherwitch in the bulrushes, yet he is drawn to the river. How does he feel in these conflicting situations? All of these scenarios are accessible, relevant to the children's emotional lives and thought-provoking. They therefore suit thought-tracking.

shapes in the half-darkness. This is an important modelling activity and your words need to evoke a sense of the bear's isolation and impending doom.

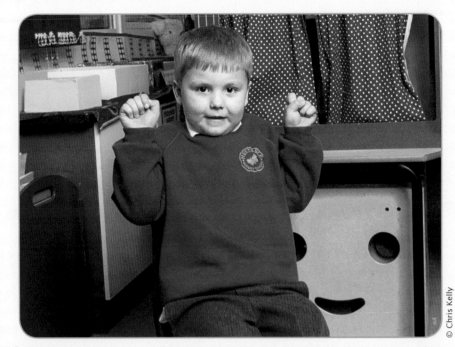
© Chris Kelly

③ Ask the children to adopt the body posture of the bear, alone on a chair in the park. Show them the picture again to help them to do this, and adopt the position yourself.

④ Say you are going to count down from five to one, and then you will all 'think out loud' together what the bear is thinking. Explain that while you will be voicing his thoughts at the same time, it should be quietly to yourselves as if you were the bear talking to yourself for reassurance.

⑤ Now put these thoughts in context. As their narrator, retell the tale or re-read it until this point in the narrative, and focus on the plight of this character. Then voice some of his views again and count down – *five, four, three, two, one*. Alternatively, you could encourage volunteers to voice their thoughts individually. Set up a chair to be touched or an object, such as a soft toy bear, to be picked up. Explain that when someone wants to speak he or she should touch the chair, or pick up the item, and that everyone else must be quiet and listen to the speaker.

⑥ Join in yourself, simultaneously tuning in to the children's voices and intervening to stop the thought-tracking when appropriate.

⑦ Ask the children to share with one another some of the things they voiced as part of the bear's thinking.

⑧ Using a simple illustration of the bear and thought bubbles to encapsulate his thoughts, record some of the children's sentences on the flipchart.

⑨ Invite the children to work individually to write in role as the bear, recording his thoughts and feelings.

⑩ Let the children draw thought bubbles around their words and use these to create a display of that moment in the text. Photographs of the children in role as the bear would enrich this display.

Moving on

● You could extend this work into diary writing from the character's perspective of the events in the narrative, enriched by the feelings voiced at that moment.

● You might create freeze-frames of the main events in the narrative and then touch one of the characters (probably the main character) from each group on the arm. Invite the child to think out loud what the character feels at that moment. In this way, the story is 'retold' from this character's point of view.

Will you be my friend?

The purpose of this activity is to help the children to identify and empathise with characters in familiar stories. It will enable them to learn to speculate about how characters might behave and feel. They will begin to be able to create simple profiles, enhancing the text they have met in the story with familiar information and experiences from their own lives. This will support them in understanding authorial devices used to create characters and will give them an opportunity to make connections between the stories and their own lives. At this stage of development it is important to help children to make explicit links with their own experiences so that they are motivated to become involved in literacy activities.

'Friendship' is a theme that all young children can understand and is significant in their lives.

Literature links

For this activity it is important to allow the children free access to the book supply in their classroom, so they can browse before making their choices. These suggested titles all have strong main characters with whom the children can make connections:

- *Clarice Bean* titles – Lauren Child (Orchard Books)
- *Wilfrid Gordon McDonald Partridge* – Mem Fox (Puffin)
- *Dear Greenpeace* – Simon James (Walker Books)
- *Owl Babies* – Martin Waddell (Walker Books)
- *This Is the Bear* series – Sarah Hayes (Walker Books)
- *Rover* – Michael Rosen (Bloomsbury Children's Books)
- *Little Lumpty* – Miko Imai (Walker Books)
- *Where's My Teddy?* – Jez Alborough (Walker Books).

What to do

1. To model this activity, choose a book with a choice of characters in, for example *Owl Babies* by Martin Waddell, and read or retell the story, sharing the illustrations with the children.

2. Discuss the three owl characters with the class. Question the children and invite responses about the individual

© Chris Kelly

characteristics of each owl. Which one do they think is brave?

3 Choose one of the characters and draw an outline on the board or flipchart to represent that character, for example a small owl to represent Bill in *Owl Babies*.

4 Discuss with the children what Bill is like, based on their knowledge of the story. For example, they may say he is small and frightened. Write these descriptions inside the outline drawn on the board.

5 Talk to the children about how befriending Bill could help him, and write their suggestions around the outside of the outline.

6 Invite the children, in pairs, to choose their own character to befriend from the owls in the story. Encourage the children to establish what they know about this particular character.

7 Ask the children to take the role of the character and the friend, for example, Bill and his friend, and to talk about Bill's problems and how the friend can help.

8 Using small whiteboards ask the children, in pairs, to draw the charcter's outline and annotate it in the same way you did, writing what they know of the character inside and how they can help outside.

9 Create an opportunity for children to browse through a range of appropriate stories, which you have previously selected for their strong characters. These could perhaps be grouped in boxes or baskets for children to share and discuss.

© Derek Cooknell

10 In pairs, give the children time to choose a story with one character that they would like to befriend. Invite the children to tell each other why they have chosen that particular character, giving two reasons.

11 Ask the children to draw, either individually or in pairs, a picture of themselves playing with their new friend. Encourage them to annotate their picture.

12 Create a display of the children's drawings, with the children's own labelling of the story character and their annotations.

Moving on

● Retell the story, or part of the story, including the children in the role of the friend of the main character.

● Add a prequel to the story, introducing how you met the character and became friends.

● Ask the children with whom they would most like to swap places in a story. Encourage them to draw a storyboard with themselves included in the action.

I need a home

This activity is designed to help children match characters and character elements with familiar settings, for example, dragons, witches and monsters with caves, or bears with forests. The children will be required to think specifically about the nature of the characters in stories they know well and to match these with conventional story settings. In addition, this activity will provide children with the opportunity to reflect on explicit, conventional characterisation in their favourite stories and to identify key themes with which they are associated.

© Early Learning Centre, www.elc.co.uk

Literature links

A bank of stories with traditional settings and one key strong character will help children with this activity. Picture books, for example *The Paper Bag Princess* by Robert Munsch (Scholastic), *Where's My Teddy?* by Jez Alborough (Walker Books) and *Owl Babies* by Martin Waddell (Walker Books), would be appropriate as they clearly identify a character with a particular setting. Versions of traditional tales could be used, including *The Three Little Wolves and the Big Bad Pig* by Eugene Trivizas and Helen Oxenbury (Egmont Children's Books) or an original version of, for example, 'Little Red Riding Hood'. A number and range of books are needed, all of which should be familiar to the children.

What to do

❶ Use enlarged pictures of 'home' settings, such as, castles, palaces, forests, cottages, caves and so on, either on the overhead projector or traced on the whiteboard from a projection. These should be accessible to the children throughout the activity, so it may be useful to have them displayed for the duration of this work.

❷ Discuss the stories that might be set in these places, drawing on tales the children know well and that have been shared in class. You may want to write them on large Post-it Notes, and attach them to the appropriate pictures.

❸ Look at characters who might fit these settings. You may want to use story props, such as puppets or toys commerically designed and marketed to represent characters in books. As you show the figures, ask the children to describe the perfect story-book home for them. For example, show a knight, who would live in a castle. Write some of these characters' names on Post-it Notes and attach them to the appropriate settings. (For a selection of these kind of toys, you could try the bookseller Madeleine Lindley Ltd at www.madeleine lindley.com.)

④ Now give the children time to select one setting, for example a palace or a cottage. They could work together in small groups or in pairs. Then ask them to think of and list as many characters as possible, both 'good' and 'bad', that might inhabit the setting. For example, a palace may contain a king, a queen and a court jester. Encourage them to refer to the class display, as appropriate.

⑤ Ask the groups to discuss and note some of the main characteristics of the figures they have listed. For example, if they are looking at a cottage setting, Grandma might be old and kindly; a witch might be wicked and nasty to children; bears might be hard working, friendly and not used to sharing.

⑥ Give each of the children a small sheet of paper or thin card (about A5 size) to make a portrait frame with a simple border. Ask the children to make a portrait of one of the charcters they have looked at. If a

cottage is the selected setting, for example, then the children could choose the witch from 'Hansel and Gretel', or Grandma from 'Little Red Riding Hood' or one of the three pigs in 'The Three Little Pigs and the Big Bad Wolf'. Emphasise that you want them to show their chosen character in, or in front of, the setting in which they belong.

⑦ These pictures can then be displayed inside the enlarged images of the settings, in the style of a portrait gallery, for instance. Some children might like to add their own picture-frame border, in which case give them blank A5 paper or card.

Moving on

● Give the children some character portraits, recreated from favourite stories, and ask them to create an ideal home for the character, drawing and annotating them if appropriate. This could be carried out individually or in pairs, with time provided for discussion and reference to stories already known.

© Chris Kelly

Characters in the family

In this activity, the children are asked to to focus on characters they know in their own families. Starting with the familiar will help children find ways to write well using characterisation. This will lead to understanding how to write realistic characters in their own story narratives. Children will enjoy discussions about their family and comparing character traits. We know that children find ideas and inspiration for their stories from the people in their own lives. Therefore, this is a rich source that needs to be mined as often as possible. The texts that are suggested here draw on the traditions of Afro-Caribbean British life. Reflect upon the use of language, make comparisons with other dialects the children have come across, and take advantage of the cultural mix in your class. The content of the children's writing can be the most demanding part of composition, but all children have a knowledge of people and events, allowing them to create great stories.

What to do

1 Read a short story or a poem about a member of the family. Try 'Granny Granny Please Comb My Hair' by Grace Nichols from *The Puffin Book of Fantastic First Poems* edited by June Crebbin, or the counting book *One Smiling Grandma* by Ann Marie Linden and Lynne Russell.

2 Allow plenty of time for discussion about the text. Encourage the children to talk about any memories that the text evokes.

Literature links

There are many texts (poems can be useful as well as stories) that deal with family life. Remember that not all children will relate to a particular family type, so include a selection of books with families from different backgrounds and cultures. Grace Nichols' poem 'Granny Granny Please Comb My Hair' can be found in *The Puffin Book of Fantastic First Poems*, edited by June Crebbin. Other 'family' books include *One Smiling Grandma* by Ann Marie Linden and Lynne Russell (Mammoth), which has vivid and engaging illustrations; *Clarice Bean, That's Me!* by Lauren Child (Orchard Books), a book rich in great family characters, and *Handa's Surprise* by Eileen Browne (Walker Books), which is a wonderful story for younger children.

One Smiling Grandma

ANN MARIE LINDEN   LYNNE RUSSELL

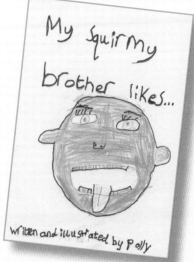

My squirmy brother has 7 girl friends.

My squirmy brother hates vegetables.

③ Ask the children to talk about their grandparents. What do they enjoy doing? What do they not enjoy doing? For example, *My Grandma likes to hug me. My Grandma dislikes roast beef. My Grandpa watches EastEnders with me and my mum.* Create opportunities for discussion and write a list on the board of the grandparents' likes and dislikes. Remember to be sensitive to individual children's circumstances – you may have to substitute an alternative family member, friend or carer for some.

④ Tell the children they are going to make a small book of what their grandma or grandpa (or other family member) likes and what makes her or him happy. You may wish the children to structure their books in a repetitive way to create a strong rhythm. For example, each page could start: *I love my grandma, she likes...*

⑤ Give the children plenty of paper, all the same size, and ask them to carefully write out their stories.

⑥ Make the books look good by sewing the leaves into the cover or using good quality staples. Allow the children to decorate the cover, referring to the books you used at the start of the activity for inspiration. If you do not have time to create these books, ask your teaching assistant to help or organise a book-making group, inviting parents to show off their skills.

Moving on

● You could ask the children to make their books rhyme, but this will depend on the age and experience of the children. There is a danger that over-emphasising the structure will have a detrimental effect upon the quality of the composition, so you will need to use your judgement as to what will best suit your class.

● You might invite the children to illustrate their books. Look at a variety of pictures from different sources for inspiration. Give the children a variety of materials – crayons, felt-tipped pens, paints and so on – and encourage the children to be as creative as they can.

● Once completed, the children could read from their books out loud in class. The children may also wish to accompany their readings with musical instruments – this will help with the rhythm of the reading and can also make a good interactive performance.

● Make a class display of all the books or, alternatively, let the children take their book home and give it to the relevant family member.

Character ladders

Children's individual responses to the characters in books are important and valid, and this activity is designed to encourage children to form their own opinions. When we, as accomplished readers, read, we constantly ask ourselves questions about the characters in the stories. We make decisions about their traits and judge if we like them or not. We do this without thinking, but some children will have to be guided as to what happens in our minds when we read, so they can understand the attractions of the journey through a book. In addition to this, discussion of characters will assist the children when creating and describing their own characters in their written compositions. It is vital that children are immersed in the characters in stories and discussion around these characters. This activity is also a convenient way to finish a story reading, and can take place quickly, but effectively.

Literature links

Any text from any media that makes use of rich characterisation can be applied successfully for this activity. Suitable books include *Clarice Bean, That's Me!* by Lauren Child (Orchard Books), *Owl Babies* by Martin Wadell (Walker Books) and *Football Crazy* by Colin McNaughton (Mammoth). A retelling of a traditional story, such as 'Wee Meg Barnileg' (page 86) and 'The Big Wide-mouthed Toad-frog' (page 88) would also work well. You might find animal stories particularly appropriate. As an alternative to books, a clip from a film shown in shared reading or writing time makes a welcome change, and the process and skills being learned are essentially the same. Disney's *Toy Story* and *Finding Nemo*, and 20th Century Fox's *Ice Age,* are full of interesting characters and the children will probably be familiar with the film. Recognition and familiarity will help to motivate the children in the learning process. *Ice Age* has some very good representations of character – Sid the Sloth is someone we we can all relate to at times! *Finding Nemo* has affecting characters in easily identifiable situations. *Toy Story 1* and *2* are also packed with a variety of clearly defined and well-loved characters.

© Chris Kelly

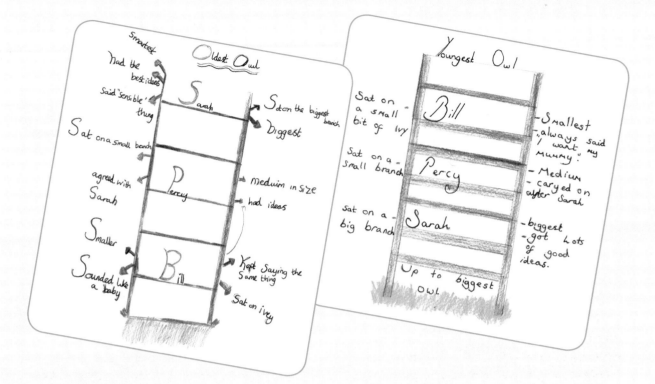

What to do

1. Together read a good quality children's story, or watch a DVD or video clip. Invite the children to help you pick a category that they felt applied to several of the characters. The categories can include: the bravest, the silliest, the cleverest, the trickiest, the most believable or the funniest. Then draw a simple ladder on the flipchart and ask the children to help you arrange on its rungs the characters they felt most fitted the chosen category.

2. Explain that you will write down one opinion on the ladder, but that other viewpoints are also valid. Scribe the name of the character that most fits the chosen description at the top of the ladder. Then work down the rungs, filling in the names of the other characters in descending order of relevance.

3. Listen to the children's suggestions, encouraging discussion and celebrating the diversity of opinions with regards to the characters. Remind the children to give you an explanation of why they think a particular character fits on the ladder where he or she does, making reference to the story.

4. Once the children are familiar with the activity, ask them to continue in pairs, drawing their own ladders and writing in the appropriate characters' names, according to the chosen description.

5. Invite the children to compare their list with others in the class, and to give reasons for their ladder's order, referring to the story wherever possible. Encourage the children to be aware that individual responses to characters may vary and that they are all equally valid.

Moving on

- To develop this activity, you could brainstorm around a class-made ladder, asking the children for words that describe the character on the top of the ladder in more detail. The children will need to explain their choices to construct these ladders.

- Weave descriptive ideas together to make a pen portrait of the character as a shared writing activity. Remember to voice the thoughts of the writer while you scribe, modelling the process, which will involve crossing out and making and correcting mistakes.

Understanding Mister Wolf

The aim of this activity is to help young children to recognise features of familiar characters in favourite stories. It will also help them to empathise with characters, and begin to understand the ways in which characters can be created to interact with each other and impact on the structure of the story. Young children will then be able to define in more detail the characters they construct for themselves. Frequently, in children's stories for this age group, characters are simply portrayed as good and gentle and kind, or bad and frightening. Exploring the characters in these ways will enable children to get to know, and eventually to predict, the nature of the stories and a character's behaviour. Later, children can manipulate these features to subvert or juxtapose characteristics. A good example of this is Lauren Child's *Beware of the Storybook Wolves* (Hodder Children's Books).

Literature links

Traditional tales can initially be used for this activity, as they have familiar, strong characters with easily identifiable features, traits and emotions. For example, stories with recognisable characters, such as the Wolf or Red Riding Hood, Jack or the Giant, the Big Bad Wolf or the last Little Pig, the Troll or the third Billy Goat Gruff could be the focus. Colin McNaughton's stories about Preston Pig in *Oops!* and *Suddenly!* (both Picture Lions) could also be used. It will be more beneficial to the children if books with rich characters are employed while they establish knowledge about characterisation in these early stages. Look for characters that are particularly engaging, funny, frightening, well described and vividly realised. In contemporary picture books, the Bear or Freddy in Jez Alborough's books *Where's My Teddy?* and *It's the Bear* (both Walker Books), or the Bear or the Boy in Sarah Hayes' *This Is the Bear and the Scary Night* (Walker Books), would provoke interesting discussions and decisions about characters.

Colin McNaughton
Oops!
A Preston Pig Story

What to do

❶ Read or retell your chosen story, for example *Oops!* by Colin McNaughton. Discuss the story with the children, allowing them time for questions, comments and responses.

❷ Talk about one of the main characters, for example Mister Wolf in *Oops!*

❸ In pairs, ask the children to think of two words to describe him. Give prompts as necessary, for example, *cunning*, *scary* and *determined*.

④ Draw around the shape of a child in the class. The back of a roll of wallpaper is ideal for this. Remember to make two of these, as you will be discussing a second character from the story later. Explain that this figure represents the character the children have been discussing. It is not important if the shape doesn't look like the character you are discussing.

⑤ Write the children's words to describe the character on large Post-it Notes or small strips of card, or ask the children to do this. Invite them to stick the words inside the character shape.

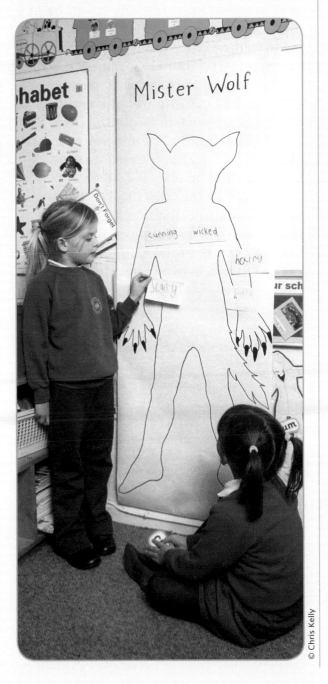
© Chris Kelly

⑥ Read the words displayed and ask the children to remember parts of the story where the character behaves in the described manner, for example, when is he particularly cunning? This will generate a retelling of the story's events, but not necessarily in the correct order. Revisit the text to confirm the children's retelling.

⑦ Identify a second significant character from the story, one that could be described as the opposite of your first character. For example, if a 'bad' character, such as Mister Wolf, was the initial focus, choose a 'good' character, such as Preston Pig. Work through the descriptive process in the same way.

Moving on

● Give the children cards on which to draw a small picture of any other characters in the story (for example, Mum, Granny or Daddy from *Oops!*). Ask them to add a word or a phrase to indicate the relationship with the main character (Mister Wolf) and their feelings about him. For example, Daddy who wants to kill him, Granny who is frightened of him, and Preston who does not know he is there. These could be displayed around the main character figure representing Mister Wolf.

● The children could create their own character outlines, annotated in this way with descriptive vocabulary. Initially, it would be better to use conventional forms of traditional tales, where characters fall easily into categories of good or evil. As children become more experienced, subversions of traditional tales could be introduced to them, to suggest ways in which characters can be changed or in which humour could be added, for example, *Lazy Jack* by Tony Ross (Andersen Press), or *The True Story of the Three Little Pigs* by Jan Scieszka (Puffin).

Character pockets

This activity endeavours to encourage the children to make an in-depth examination of a character. It approaches this area of writing in an unusual way, and is a great deal of fun, connecting with children on a personal level. By asking them to think about the contents of a character's pockets, the children will begin to think deeply about

Literature links

The best stories are full of interesting characters that can be discussed and shared. Children always love *The Julian Stories* by Ann Cameron (Corgi). The two characters get themselves into all sorts of scrapes and tend to react in a predictable fashion, which young children begin to recognise and enjoy. *Mr Cosmo the Conjuror* by Allan Ahlberg (Puffin) and *Dr Dog* by Babette Cole (Red Fox) are simple stories with engaging characters, which can be discussed. *Herb, The Vegetarian Dragon* by Jules Bass (Barefoot) introduces the concept of not eating meat as well as portraying a rather lovely dragon.

personality and motivation. Children always carry strange things around in their pockets, which are linked to their own personalities. Initially it will be necessary to prompt the children to refer to the text to support their comments and opinions, but after a while this will become automatic. Once children have considered different characters, they will begin to write convincing details in their own character portraits. A good starting point for this activity would be a discussion of the items the children like to have with them at all times, thus making a useful a connection between the fictional characters and the children's own experiences.

What to do

1. Choose a character from a book you have been reading to the children – it might be Huey from *The Julian Stories*, for example, or Dr Dog. Ask the children to discuss, in pairs, what Huey would always carry around with him in his pockets. This may be an elastic band, some chewing gum or a toy Buzz Lightyear. Dr Dog may have a thermometer and medicines.

2. Ask the children to note down their ideas. Don't worry about spelling as the children are making notes – which will not be shown to anyone else – and spending too much time on transcription will impede their ideas. Imagination is more important than presentation here.

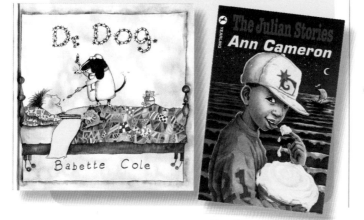

❸ Invite the children to share their ideas with the class. List some of these on the flipchart.

❹ Ask the children why they think the character carries these items. Add their reasons to the flipchart. This is a good opportunity to really discuss the character. Allow the children to offer ideas about the characters that draw on their own experiences of the world as well as the text. These contributions should be personal, and with the character of Huey or Dr Dog, they will be warmly funny.

❺ Ask the children to illustrate the character and write a sentence to briefly describe what he or she has in their pockets.

Moving on

● Invite the children to draw a character to include in their own story. Ask them to explain, in the style of a labelled diagram, why their character is wearing certain clothing, their haircut, their shoes and what they keep in their pockets. Drawing can be a rich source of ideas for stories and helps children to relate play activities to the play involved in creating characters.

● Encourage the children to write a story about their character that draws on the work they have been doing. They should include some of the detail shown in their pictures. The articles found in the pockets of their characters will have stories attached to them. An elastic band may be from a set of trading cards stolen by the school bully, or a fossil may have been found on a camping holiday in the West Country.

Shaking out characters

This activity helps children to identify significant characters in stories and the behaviour that sums them up. It will encourage children to examine key themes that relate to certain characters. Above all, this is a playful activity that will motivate children to explore picture fiction and use their existing knowledge of stories.

Literature links

Any books with strong, active characters, such as *Beware of the Storybook Wolves* by Lauren Child (Hodder Children's Books), *The Demon Teddy* by Nicholas Allan (Red Fox), *The Paper Bag Princess* by Robert Munsch (Scholastic), *The Rascally Cake* by Jeanne Willis (Puffin) *and Dr Dog* by Babette Cole (Red Fox) could all be used to good effect. Humorous stories can be particularly useful for character study at this level.

What to do

❶ Prepare a selection of paper cut-outs of story characters known to the children.

❷ Read your chosen story. *Beware of the Storybook Wolves* by Lauren Child is ideal as it uses the device of 'shaking' characters out of one book to help in another book.

❸ Discuss the ways in which this story makes reference either directly or indirectly to other stories.

❹ Discuss why the Fairy Godmother was chosen to shake out of the book. For example, she was experienced, had powerful magic and knew about wolves. Mention other traditional stories with fairy godmothers, such as 'Cinderella'. Help the children to appreciate the comic effects.

❺ Assist the children, in pairs, to identify books which contain useful characters.

❻ Gather the class together and shake out your simple cut-out characters. Ask why these might be useful, for example, are they are cunning or kind? List these qualities on the flipchart.

❼ In pairs, ask the children to shake one of these characters into one of their own favourite stories, to change the course of the narrative. Share some of the retellings.

❽ During shared or guided writing, support the children in rewriting a section of the text with the inclusion of a new character.

Moving on

● Use character cut-outs in a 'character pot' as a story-making resource.

● Use a well-known character from comics or television and place him or her in an unlikely story to change the action, for example, Bart Simpson could be put into 'Cinderella' or Dennis the Menace into 'Little Red Riding Hood'.

Chapter Three

Story Settings

p52   Through the magic mirror

p54   Making story worlds

p56   Drawing a setting

p58   Picture poems

p60   Photographs

p62   Let's make the place

p64   Place the story

Identifying where stories are set and understanding the reasons for this, are significant stages on the journey to becoming an independent reader and writer. Young children are accustomed to creating imaginary story worlds in their play and to transforming commonplace situations into fantasy worlds. So it can actually be a small step for children to take, from these concrete situations in their play worlds, to imaginary settings in stories.

Suspending reality and stepping from the classroom to an exotic island, for example, can be easily undertaken during shared times by employing drama techniques, as in the activity 'Through the magic mirror'. Initially, this sort of work will need to be supported and developed by an energetic and creative teacher. Although children quickly begin to mirror activities like this in their own independent play situations and add fantastic elements to basic story settings. It is still apparent, though, the more that high quality stories are read or told to children, the greater the repertoire they have for creating their own story worlds.

Computer console games and television have helped even very young children at the beginning of Key Stage 1 to have a broad sense of the richness and diversity of the world they live in, and the world of stories. Even though these two worlds often overlap in the minds of children, the connections they are able to make, and the differences they are able to identify between their lived-in worlds and the worlds of others, provide the beginnings of story construction and story writing. Indeed, television has presented children, from toddlers upwards, with pictures and the potential for imagining. The technology of computers has given children further opportunities to take ownership of designing, defining and shaping settings and adventures for characters in this medium. Even the youngest children, at the pre-school stage, are very often given unlimited access to television and computer games, and so already have heads full of landscapes and images, often lurid and colourful, in which to set their own imaginary stories.

Children often come into school then with a knowledge of settings gleaned from television and computers, combined perhaps with more traditional aspects of storytelling and reading. Given this rich diversity of experience, activities such as 'Drawing a setting' or 'Photographs' provide the children with opportunities to think about their own lives, talk about experiences and be supported in using appropriate language to describe places they know or have seen.

In school, children will encounter an even greater range of high quality picture books and illustrated texts than they have at home. Frequently used settings in picture books include castles, the seaside and woods, as well as familiar places, such as bedrooms, homes and parks. Books, such as *This Is the Bear* by Sarah Hayes (Walker Books) or *A Walk in the Park* (Hamish Hamilton) and *Voices in the Park* (Corgi) by Anthony Browne, and the *Percy the Park Keeper* series by Nick Butterworth (Collins), can be grouped together and combined with children's own experiences of parks to carry out activities described in this chapter, such as 'Picture poems'. Books containing bears and woodland are frequently seen in Key Stage 1 classrooms. The Jez Alborough series, starting with *It's the Bear* (Walker Books) are great favourites, but illustrated versions of fairy stories such as 'Goldilocks and the Three Bears', still often familiar from home, could also be included in this collection.

Classrooms for Reception and Key Stage 1 are always visually stimulating and will echo children's out-of-school experiences, as well as the settings they encounter in the fictional worlds of stories. Thus, the work which teachers do in supporting children's understanding of settings fits naturally into their existing experiences. Pictures and posters depicting places will extend the work of the books that children encounter. However, the enormous range of high quality picture books now available to children enables them to have their own worlds mirrored, challenged, or another place offered in

© photodisc. inc.

complete contrast. Maurice Sendak, in *Where the Wild Things Are* (Red Fox), helps children to dip in and out of familiar places, offering security and challenge in a short space of time. As does Anthony Browne in *A Walk in the Park* (Hamish Hamilton) or Ralph Steadman in *That's My Dad* (Andersen Press) or Sally Grindley in *Knock Knock Who's There?* (Puffin). These books provide a safe starting point for children, echoing what they already know, and then moving them on. This means questions and problems are immediately encountered to help them as developing readers and writers.

© Image 100 Ltd

Books written for young children are often multi-layered, thereby allowing children with varied levels of experience to meet the text just where they are able to without feeling any sense of failure. For example, in *Knock Knock Who's There?* by Sally Grindley (Puffin), the children will be supported by seeing the familiar setting of a bedroom, which will draw them into the text, but then the fantastic takes over as unreal characters are juxtaposed with this ordinary place. As children become writers, they are then able to lean on this model to create settings from their own experience in which to place characters they have imagined. Another good example of this is *Rover* by Michael Rosen (Bloomsbury Children's Books), which sets its action at a seaside that even many very young and inexperienced children will recognise and be interested in, and takes its action through places that they will probably know well. Yet there is also another layer of meaning, which will challenge more experienced readers and amuse adults.

Other books we have used in the activities in this chapter include:

- **Smelly Jelly, Smelly Fish** – Michael Rosen (Walker Books)
- **We're Going on a Bear Hunt** – Michael Rosen (Walker Books)
- **The Smallest Whale** – Elisabeth Beresford (Orchard)

Of course, computer technology is available in school now. Sophisticated software, talking books and some of the commercially-produced story texts on disk that link with print versions, for example, *The Fish Who Could Wish* by John Bush (Oxford University Press), are an additional and useful method to enable children to craft and shape settings to influence, change or subvert the story.

In school there are also opportunities to use the simplest materials to help children to construct story worlds. A variety of props, music and perhaps just an indication of an undersea world or a castle turret in the role-play area, will facilitate the journey from a classroom to an imaginary setting. Much of the children's story making at this stage will be oral. Children will most effectively work out and negotiate where stories are to take place in the company of other children and through talk. It is also appropriate that the crafting of setting, the use of descriptive vocabulary and the shaping of story action, will occur through physical activity. Children should be encouraged to use small-world equipment, sand, water, big blocks, large paper and felt-tipped pens, play dough, role-play areas and outside space to construct their story settings.

The joy of supporting work on story settings, particularly with this age group, is that it can be playful, dramatic, engaging, self-motivating, inclusive, collaborative and fun!

Through the magic mirror

In this imaginative drama activity, the children are invited 'into' a familiar setting. They are encouraged to think about the aspects of this place, employing all of their senses. Acting out miniature scenes will inspire the children to think of words to describe the setting, which they will then be able to use in a written composition.
For this activity to be successful, teachers need to be able to model role-play, and to create a sense of playful drama to enable children to understand and engage in the experience. Children do, of course, spend a great deal of time in other worlds created by their imaginations, so the activity will not be unusual – with the exception that the teacher is now asking them to do it! The process of writing a good setting will involve the author entering the world in their heads. This activity shows children how to do this and, most importantly, that they have been doing it everyday for most of their lives. A significant aspect of this activity is that the setting will, in most cases, be familiar to them.

What to do

❶ Read a good quality picture book that has a similar setting to the one you wish the children to discuss. For the seaside try *Smelly Jelly, Smelly Fish* by Michael Rosen, illustrated by Quentin Blake.

❷ After the reading, inform the children that they are going to imagine they are all going to the seaside. To do this, the children need to step through the 'magic mirror'. You will need to stand up and, with your finger, draw the shape of a large mirror in the air. Wink an eye and step through. Tell the children that this is how to go to the imaginary seaside.

❸ The children will need to take their white boards, because you want them to record what it is like there. Tell them to pack two other (imaginary) items for the trip and ask them to share these items with their neighbour.

Literature links

All four of these books are great fun and also involve a variety of settings. The first three have patterned and predictable texts. *Smelly Jelly, Smelly Fish* by Michael Rosen (Walker Books) is set at the seaside. *We're Going on a Bear Hunt*, also by Michael Rosen (Walker Books), has an exciting adventure for the children to follow. *Click Clack Moo: Cows That Type* by Doreen Cronin (Simon and Schuster) and *'Mind Me Good Now!'* by Lynette Commisiong (Annick Press) also offer rich settings.

④ Let the children stand and draw their mirrors. Ask them to wink and step through. Say that they are now at the seaside and should take a deep breath. What can they smell?

⑤ Explain to the children that they need to report back on their seaside world by writing on their white boards. First, ask them to give you some examples of what they can smell, then encourage the children to write these down.

⑥ Ask them to look to the left, then to the right and straight ahead – what can they see? Finally, what can they hear? After each question, the children should jot down some ideas on their white boards. There is no need, at this stage, to worry about spellings – after all, there's no dictionaries at the seaside!

⑦ Ask the children to go and collect three (imaginary) items that they can see which can be picked up. Encourage the children to show the objects and describe them to their neighbour – can their neighbour tell what it is from their description? Share examples with the whole class.

⑧ Now ask the children to do what they like to do best at the seaside. Ask them to create a freeze-frame when you say so and hold their position. Invite a couple of children to hold their position again while the rest of the class guess what they are doing.

⑨ Let the children gather the items they have found on the beach and come back through the magic mirror. Remind them to wink before they step through.

⑩ Sit the children down and collect the words they wrote on their white boards that describe the seaside. Weave them together in a shared writing activity.

© Chris Kelly

Moving on

● Ask the children to write down their own descriptions of the seaside for a story they will write with this setting. Share some of their work, and with the child's permission, critique one example with the class, demonstrating how first drafts can be improved either in terms of composition or transcription, but not both at the same time. We know from research that concentrating on both composition and transcription at the same time will impede both these parts of the writing process. A good copy can always be made later on if the work is to be presented.

● This drama activity can be used for a variety of settings, linking in with the type of story narrative you are teaching, for example, traditional tales.

Making story worlds

The purpose of this activity is to provide children with an opportunity to physically create settings of stories that they have been introduced to and are familiar with. Through working in this 'hands-on' way with story resources, children are able to re-enact stories while shaping the setting in which the action takes place. As children are used to creating their own settings and directing the action around this when they are playing, making decisions in such self-directed playful activities will not be unfamiliar or daunting to them. Naturally, at this stage of development, the children's working and shaping of the story will be mainly through talk, with key moments tracked through the materials they are using and the constructions that they make.

What to do

❶ Read or retell a favourite journey story, such as *We're Going on a Bear Hunt* by Michael Rosen (Walker Books).

❷ Provide time for the children to comment on, and respond to the story, perhaps repeating the refrains together, in order to take the children into the story. This is a

Literature links

With the youngest children in this age group, the use of nursery rhymes is appropriate and these can be supported by texts, such as *Once Upon a Time* by Vivian French and John Prater (Walker Books) and *Each Peach Pear Plum* by Janet and Allan Ahlberg (Puffin). Other books, which will support this work on settings, include those that have a journey in them, such as *We're Going on a Bear Hunt* (Walker Books) and *Rover* (Bloomsbury Children's Books), both by Michael Rosen. In these stories the action is sequenced through a range of different settings that can be easily identified and recreated by young children. Of course oral stories, such as 'Wee Meg Barnileg' (page 86) and 'The Big Wide-mouthed Toad-frog' (page 88), also have clear structures, as the characters move through places where events occur. This will help the children in understanding the structure and in remembering the story themselves for retelling.

good opportunity to model intonation and expression so that the children gather a sense of excitement and anticipation.

❸ Ask the children to remember each step of the journey. See if they can do it in order. List the steps on the board, for example, through the long wavy grass, through the deep cold river, through the thick oozy mud, and so on.

© Delta of Sweden www.deltasand.net

❹ Using materials you have available, such as a small tidy tray filled with damp sand, discuss and model with the children how these art/craft/ modelling materials could be used to represent stages of the journey. In this case, you could burrow and building up, making river beds and oozy mud and creating a cave. Take suggestions from the children and tell them that when they have a go at representing the story in this way you will want them to be inventive. They can even digress from the original story, perhaps creating additional hazards on the journey, such as the addition of a busy road full of cars. However, make sure you and the children keep to the bones of the story and remember the refrain *We can't go over it. We can't go under it...*

❺ Divide the children into pairs or groups. Give each group one of a variety of resources to create the setting, or the journey through a range of settings, for example, a sand tray, the role-play area, the puppet theatre, or a large sheet of paper and fat, coloured felt-tipped pens. Initially, allocate the children to specific resources, although as they become more experienced in this kind of playful activity, the resources could be made available for them to choose from. This experimentation could take place either in the Literacy Hour as an independent activity, or during a literacy activity time, replacing quiet reading.

❻ Ask the children, in their pairs or small groups, to recreate the places they remembered from the story, using the given resource and any other available materials. Encourage the children to revisit the story to support their work, and to retell the story as they go along.

❼ Use the plenary for the children to talk about the setting they created, reviewing it and celebrating any new additional places they made to enhance the journey.

Moving on

● A display could be made from the children's work, with the name of the book and any other information about the setting written as annotation.

● Take photographs with a digital camera, and use these to recreate the story on screen as well as on a display, using the children's own retellings, independently or teacher scribed.

Drawing a setting

This activity involves children using their imagination through drawing to create a setting for a story narrative they will then go on to write. Children love to draw and are constantly illustrating scenes in which stories take place. When children are asked to describe their pictures they will often orally tell the story of their drawing. This activity utilises this skill and assists the children in converting their drawings into written form. Much of the composition that will later be developed into writing has already been done at the drawing stage. Therefore, the children will not be left with the burdensome task of writing from scratch. Instead, they work and build upon the setting and the story within the picture they have drawn. The scene the children are asked to draw may be from a setting related to a type of story already worked on in class –settings from fairy stories, familiar settings and so on. It could equally be a setting of the child's own choosing. Essentially, it simply needs to be a picture of a place.

Literature links

This activity has potential for a number of story types that you may be teaching. There are many good picture books where the illustrator has contributed to the storytelling by doing wonderful pictures. *The Snoops* written by Miriam Moss and illustrated by Delphine Durand (Templar) has intriguing illustrations of street life. *The Lost Thing* by Shaun Tan (Lothian) is a demanding picture book that can be used as a stimulus for discussion. *Changes* by Anthony Browne (Walker Books) has settings changing before the reader's eyes. *Some Things Are Scary* written by Florence Parry Heide and illustrated by Jules Feiffer (Walker Books) has a number of funny, but scary, settings.

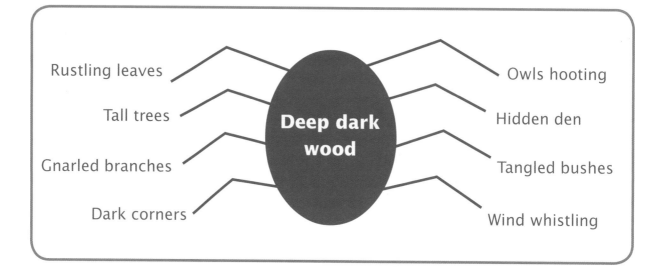

What to do

❶ Ask the children to draw a picture, perhaps based on the kind of settings they have been studying for a unit of work. It does not have to be a particular scene from a book, but it might be a setting typical of a genre – a deep dark wood, or a world of complete fantasy, for example. Ensure that stimulating resources are provided for this drawing, including felt-tipped pens, crayons and good-sized paper. This will lead to a special piece of writing.

❷ Go round the class, talking quietly to individual children. Ask them to describe their scene to you as they are drawing. This could be a good opportunity for you to assess how the children cope with telling a tale and the different literary conventions they are able to use.

Moving on

● You could ask small groups of children to describe their setting as part of a guided writing activity. This will give you a better opportunity to assist the children with the language and the organisation of their description. Intensive, direct teaching is the main benefit of guided writing and gives greater opportunity for the teacher to focus on groups of children that require greater support. Remember the groups do not have to be formed because of ability.

● The pictures could be displayed alongside the writing the children have done, to illustrate the process. This is a great opportunity for making links between artwork and text. Encourage the children to describe their settings on the wall to visitors coming into the class.

❸ Once the children have finished their pictures, invite them to describe their scene to a partner. It may be necessary to move the children around, so that they can talk to someone new – someone they were not near to during the period when they were drawing.

❹ Invite one or two of the children to describe the scene to the whole class, to act as a model for everyone else.

❺ Before asking the children to write their setting, you may wish to do some further preparatory work by asking them to create a spider diagram of their setting. Each leg of the spider diagram can be used to describe a particular aspect of the scene. This should help the children to organise their writing on the page.

❻ Invite the children to write the setting as the start of an exciting story based on this scene. Give as much support as necessary to help them with their writing and be ready to praise the children's work to keep them motivated in the activity.

Picture poems

This activity invites children to draw on their own experience of settings. In a piece of shared writing, the class creates a list poem that captures a familiar setting suitable for a story. It is formed upon the premise that children are active in their own environments and are very familiar with a variety of different settings. Why ask children to think up an unknown setting when they have plenty of them in their own experiences? The children are asked to think hard about a familiar setting, generating words that describe this place in various ways. The settings children choose will often be those connected to school and home life. Their descriptions can be very useful and enlightening in helping to understand their personalities. This activity will also help children to concentrate on settings to facilitate greater attention to detail when they come to write their own stories. A glance through any modern anthology of poetry will reveal the diverse nature of poetry available these days. Definitions of what poetry is, has become increasingly blurred. What remains is the consistent playful nature of the use of words, and how poets have always reflected upon their own environment and, indeed, setting.

What to do

❶ Ask the children to think of a place they know very well – this might be a supermarket, the playground, the classroom, the dining hall, the after-school club, the doctor's or dentist's surgery. Encourage them to think of somewhere other than their house. As a group, agree on one of the suggested settings on which to focus, before you start the initial shared writing activity.

❷ Invite all the children to imagine this setting and the people in it. Noting ideas on the flip chart, ask the children to tell you all the things that are happening (verbs) in their imagined setting. For example, in the playground could be: *run, jump, shout, sing, laugh* and *cry*.

❸ At this point, to add variety to your session and to get the children fully actively engaged, ask them to create a freeze-frame/still mime of one of the activities you have noted relating to this setting. Ask for some examples to show the children. Write these (fairly small) on the flipchart, and then ask for all the things that are being said. Here, you will be asking for quotes, for example, in the playground setting: *He won't play with me, she hit me.*

Literature links

There are a number of good poetry books that depict familiar settings from a personal point of view. These books will fit in well with the children's introduction to poetry. *Quick, Let's Get Out of Here* by Michael Rosen and Quentin Blake (Puffin) is a great introduction to Rosen's poems. *Very Best (almost) Friends* collected by Paul B Janeczko (Walker Books) has the trials of friendship described by many poets. *Friendly Matches* by Allan Ahlberg (Puffin) and *Juggling With Gerbils* by Brian Patten (Puffin) both depict familiar worlds.

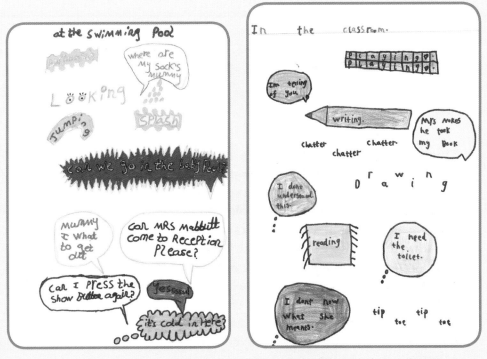

④ Then, ask for what is being thought by the people taking part in the activities, and scribe these on the flipchart, straight under the previous list. Here you will be looking for the subtle differences between spoken word and thoughts. The whole class will learn about how others are feeling in certain situations. Settings from within the school will assist the children in their empathy with others around them. Some of the issues raised around friendship and general attitudes to others in these environments can form the basis for fruitful discussions.

⑤ Lastly, ask for the noises that can be heard. You will need to try to write down the sounds as they are heard, for example: *boing, boing, boing; crunch, crunch, crunch, slap!* and may need to make up some onomatapoeic words to suit.

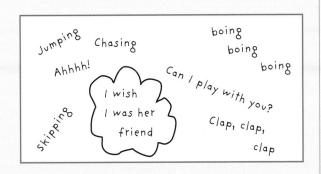

⑥ Read out the full lists of happenings, sayings, thoughts and noises with the children. This should come to be in the form of a list/picture poem of the place.

⑦ The children can then go to their tables with large pieces of paper and go through the same process to create a similar poem for another setting they know, using the same categories.

⑧ This time the children should repeat the process. However, on another occasion, or for children who have time in this session, you could ask for pictures to be drawn to illustrate the setting in addition to the description in words.

Moving on

● Ask the children to use their poems for the basis of a story, written with a partner. They could draw on the words they have used, with the feelings evoked by the speech and thoughts, to create the atmosphere for their story that takes place in this familiar setting.

● Make a display of the picture poems, with the children's illustrations to enrich the settings. Viewers can consider how good these descriptions are at illustrating the setting. Put them up in an area where adults can view them too. The thoughts of individuals in the playground or the classroom can tell adults a great deal about children's perceptions of school life.

Photographs

This activity works superbly in shared writing. It uses good quality and evocative photographs from magazines or Sunday supplements, or books that contain the work of well-respected photographers, to encourage children to describe in words a setting for a story. The children will start by studying the photograph and then be given the opportunity to generate ideas as a class. Here the planning and execution of effective descriptions of a setting can be modelled. Asking children to examine settings is one of the National Literacy Strategy objectives throughout Key Stage 1. This activity will also give a new dimension to your Literacy Hour and your whole-class sessions. Children are very experienced at 'reading' pictures. They will have a great deal to say about them. This will give you the opportunity to involve the children in the kind of productive talk that will enable them to write about settings. It helps the children to realise that they have lots of ideas and vocabulary they can use when they are writing.

Literature links

Be on the look out for colour photographs of interesting settings in Sunday supplements, travel brochures and other magazines. *National Geographic* and travel magazines such as *Wanderlust, Global* or *The Sunday Times Travel* are good places to start. You could build up a collection to use for this kind of activity. Good quality picture books often have wonderful drawings of where the story takes place. *Seasons of Splendour* by Madhur Jaffrey with illustrations by Michael Foreman (Puffin) has stunning settings. *Owl Babies* by Martin Waddell, illustrated by Patrick Benson (Walker), has a scary wood scene. Consider cities and built up areas, as well as countryside landscapes, and fantastical settings too. *The Brothers Grimm Popular Folk Tales* translated by Brian Alderson and illustrated by Michael Foreman (Hamish Hamilton) also has frightening pictures – this time they get gory! *Angus Rides the Goods Train* by Alan Durant and illustrated by Chris Riddell (Corgi) has some wonderful fantasy illustrations.

What to do

❶ Choose a photograph of a setting large enough for the children to see (you may want to put it on to an overhead transparency). The location should be a place with enough detail and interest to stimulate imagination and discussion. Ask the children to discuss, in pairs, who might live in such a setting and then to feed back to the class. Note these suggested characters on the flipchart.

❷ Again in pairs, ask the children to now think of words to describe this place – you

© Corel

will need to model the kind of words to use (adjectives) to start the children off. Write them up on the flipchart. Take this opportunity to talk about spelling strategies, spelling patterns and rules, and the use of phonics.

❸ You will then need to start turning these words into phrases, either asking the children for phrases or adding words yourself – writing them on the board as you go. You might write, for example: *A colourful and lush garden with a long hedge and a tall, green tree.* Here again you will be able to discuss writing at sentence level, looking at grammatical construction and punctuation.

❹ Agree on a selection of phrases that sound right together in terms of the setting, and begin to weave these phrases into a piece of shared writing that describes the setting provided in the picture. The children will be able to watch the construction of a text right in front of their eyes. In addition, they will see their words come together in a genuinely shared writing experience. Model the drafting process, crossing out, making changes, and finishing with a good first copy for a setting for a story.

❺ Keep the draft and the picture on display until the next session, so the children will have time to reflect on the work you have done together. If you place the work in a prominent position, the children will look at it and discuss it with you or their friends. This will help them when they are asked to go back to it.

Moving on

● The next day, return to this piece of writing and make further changes where needed. This again models the writing process.

● Provide the children with a new photograph of a setting and remind the class of the process you went through previously. Ask the children to work in pairs to describe the new setting. The skills the children have already learned can then be put into practice. By working in pairs, the children will be able to bounce ideas off each other and gain confidence in their ability.

● You might ask the children to plan and build on the setting in order to make a complete story about this place. Invite the children to work in pairs to discuss ideas about two main characters and what happens to them in this place. The children could also work together to write the story down.

Let's make the place

The purpose of this activity is to imaginatively recreate a particular setting from a book by taking on the role of the characters and objects in it. This can help young children appreciate the concept of place and develop an awareness of the importance of detail in settings. The children's full physical involvement encourages the generation and representation of ideas, and allows the resultant writing to be enriched by the dramatic improvisation.

Literature links

The most valuable books for this activity are those based mainly in a single setting of real significance to the story. *The Hidden House* by Martin Waddell (Walker Books) is set in a deserted old house, *The Fish Who Could Wish* by John Bush (OUP) has the ocean as its setting, *Tattybogle* by Sandra Horn (Hodder Children's Books) takes place outdoors, and *The Smallest Whale* by Elisabeth Beresford (Orchard) has a beach setting. Alternatively, a book with two different settings would also work, for example, *The Rainbow Bear* by Michael Morpurgo (Corgi). Picture books are most suitable for this activity as the illustrations can be examined closely and recreated through the children's imaginative involvement.

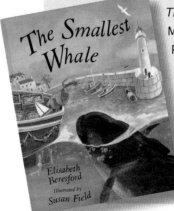

What to do

1. Show the class the front cover of a chosen book and together discuss the place in which the story is likely to be situated. It does not matter if the children know the book. For example, in discussing *The Smallest Whale* by Elisabeth Beresford (Orchard), the children may well guess that the action takes place in the ocean or by the beach.

2. Provide time for the class to talk, in pairs, about their experience of similar settings. Even if they have not been to the sea, for example, they may well have watched the video/DVD of Walt Disney's classic film, *The Little Mermaid*.

3. Read part or all of the story to the class, either stopping at a moment in the text when the setting is making an impact on the tale and when the picture visuals are very clear, or returning to this moment after reading the entire story. In *The Smallest Whale*, the whale is beached and stranded on the sand, unable to return to the water. The townsfolk gather round, at first unsure of what to do.

4. Together examine the picture closely and suggest to the class that you make the picture yourselves with your bodies and then bring it to life.

5. Identify where significant features could be in the classroom, for example, in *The Smallest Whale*, consider locations for the sea, the beach and the seafront town.

⑥ Invite pairs and small groups of children by name to create various physical elements of the scene. In effect, you are building up the setting, piece by piece, with the children using their bodies to make the components. For example, in *The Smallest Whale,* the children could create the houses, the fire engine, the pier and the ice-cream stalls.

⑦ When everyone is in position, ask them to stay still and pretend to take a photograph of the scene. (If you have a digital camera, you could take a picture to use for a display.)

⑧ Ask the children what they can smell, see, hear and touch. They could perhaps add noises to the setting too. Record their ideas on a flipchart under headings of the senses. Encourage the children to offer longer phrases as well as words to make the description more evocative, for example: *the rushing waves, the worried faces of the children, the weak breathing of the whale, the chatter of the seagulls* and so on.

⑨ Finally, remake the scene, this time populating the place with people, for example, the little boy and his father, the firefighters and the townsfolk with their chain of buckets. Be sure to include the key characters in the tale and, when everyone is in place, ask the children to bring the scene to life by improvising.

⑩ Take other pictures with an imaginary or real camera, recording the scene as you move around the class.

⑪ Look back at the book together to discuss whether you have evoked the place effectively. What might be the key feeling/ atmosphere on the beach at this point in the tale? Is it despair, or hope that the stranded whale will be saved? How can this be conveyed in the improvisation?

Moving on

● In shared writing you might create a paragraph together to describe the setting of the story, using the words listed before, and working to paint a word picture of the place, making sure the atmosphere is clear.

● In an art and design lesson, you could encourage the children to contribute to a large mural of the setting, with each group or pair responsible for making their 'own' part of the tale. Other stories with seaside settings could be displayed alongside.

© Chris Kelly

Place the story

This is a playful way of consolidating the children's understanding of the sense of place in stories, and its influence on the characters and action. The children collect a rich and descriptive form of words to prompt their peers to guess a story setting. Obviously the richer the description, the more likely children are to be able to guess and, as they become more experienced they will realise that, the more subtle their descriptions the more difficult it is to guess.

Literature links

The most appropriate books for this activity are those which are particularly descriptive in both their language and their illustration. Here are just a few suggestions: *A Dark, Dark Tale* or *Toad* by Ruth Brown (both Red Fox), *Cloudland* by John Burningham (Red Fox) and *Knock Knock Who's There?* by Sally Grindley (Puffin).

What to do

❶ Select a range of stories that emphasise a sense of place, and give the children time to look through them. Encourage the children to talk about the books while they are browsing. Invite pairs to choose a book they know well and can describe.

❷ Ask the children to focus on where the books are set, discussing those which include more than one setting, and identifying the key places in the story.

❸ Ask the children to think of words to describe the setting. It might be useful initially, depending on the experience of the class, to give the children a frame to work with. This could be written on a chart or on the overhead projector, and then the children could add to it. For example, they could begin with:

● *My book is set in... (a creepy, cheerful, beautiful...) place.*
● *At first it made me feel... (scared, happy...).*
● *It is... (dark, light, bright...).*
● *I can see... I can hear... I can touch... I can smell...*

❹ Model this for the children on the first occasion with a particularly evocative book. This will show them how they can create a sense of atmosphere through both the language they use and the expression in their voice.

❺ Invite the children, in their pairs or groups, to give their descriptions so that the rest of the children can guess the place and therefore the book.

Moving on

● This suggestion is a guessing game that children could play in pairs. Depending on the age and experience of the children, they could be allowed to work either with words or pictures. First they should each create in their minds, or on a small whiteboard which they keep hidden initially, their chosen book and place, and indicate what these are with picture clues or write simple descriptions. Then ask them to swap their boards or their ideas and guess each other's setting and book. For example, they might either say: *It's set in a jungle; it's bright and lively and there are lots of jungle animals in a circle*, or draw jungle trees and a circle of animals.

Chapter Four

Theme and Language

p68   Book-spread

p70   Mirror the theme

p72   Speaking out

p74   Advertise the film

p76   Songs, rhymes and chants

p78   'Get out of here'

p80   Washing lines

p82   Telling together

Young learners need to engage with the language and themes of a multitude of stories, before they are invited to attend to the literary turns of phrase or the key messages in a text. In the classroom, reading aloud, storytelling, using story tapes, and shared and guided reading offer significant opportunities for children to experience the language of narrative. Revisiting known texts play an important part in building up the repertoire of familiar stories, which children can draw upon as they focus on theme and language.

Theme

Young children need the opportunity to collect and discuss themes in stories, and to connect them with their own experiences to learn about their own lives. This is the main focus of the National Literary Strategy at this age. Books with common themes can be collected, displayed and used to help young children develop their awareness of theme, as in the activity 'Book-spread'. Gradually children will learn to compare and contrast the ways different authors handle the same theme.

These skills can be used to link to the children's own experiences, and personal, oral or written narratives are likely to emerge which connect to the world of fiction, as in 'Mirror the theme' activity. Children can also develop their preferences for particular themes as well as authors and illustrators in these years.

In addition to presenting and displaying texts on common themes, teachers can invite the children to contribute to these displays and ask them to identify their own books, grouped according to theme. Suggested groupings of popular Foundation and Key Stage 1 texts include the following:

© Thinkstock

Losing something
- *Dogger* – Shirley Hughes (Red Fox)
- *Where's My Teddy?* – Jez Alborough (Walker Books)
- *Owl Babies* – Martin Waddell (Walker Books)
- *Where Is Monkey?* – Dieter Schubert (Red Fox)
- *Wilfrid Gordon McDonald Partridge* – Mem Fox (Puffin)

The Dark
- *After Dark* – Louis Baum (Mammoth)
- *Can't You Sleep Little Bear?* – Martin Waddell (Walker Books)

© PhotoDisc

- *This Is the Bear and the Scary Night* – Sarah Hayes (Walker Books)
- *The Owl Who Was Afraid of the Dark* – Jill Tomlinson (Mammoth)
- *Kate's Giants* – Valiska Gregory (Walker Books)
- *I Can't Sleep* – Philippe Dupasquier (Orchard)
- *I'm Coming to Get You* – Tony Ross (Puffin)
- *The Midnight Man* – Berlie Doherty (Walker Books)

Babies
- *A Baby for Grace* – Ian Whybrow (Kingfisher)
- *Changes* – Anthony Browne (Walker Books)
- *Tell Me Again About the Night I Was Born* – Jamie Lee Curtis (HarperCollins)
- *Baby Bird* – Joyce Dunbar (Walker Books)
- *Once There Were Giants* – Martin Waddell (Walker Books)

Going away
- *The Train Ride* – June Crebbin (Walker Books)
- *Don't Forget to Write* – Martina Selway (Red Fox)
- *A Sailing Boat in the Sky* – Quentin Blake (Red Fox)
- *Willa and Old Miss Annie* – Berlie Doherty (Walker Books)
- *Little Polar Bear* – Hans de Beer (North–South Books)

Being in trouble
- *The Time It Took Tom* – Nick Sharratt and Stephen Tucker (Scholastic)
- *Oscar Got the Blame* – Tony Ross (Andersen Press)
- *John Patrick Norman McHennessy – the Boy Who Was Always Late* – John Burningham (Red Fox)
- *Do You Dare?* – Paul and Emma Rogers (Orchard)
- *Little Rabbit Foo Foo* – Michael Rosen (Walker Books)
- *This Is the Bear and the Bad Little Girl* – Sarah Hayes (Walker Books)
- *On Friday Something Funny Happened* – John Prater (Red Fox)

Language

The wealth of texts available means that teachers in the Early Years and Key Stage 1 are able to select highly patterned, predictable and rhythmic texts, recommended by the National Literacy Strategy. Many of these texts have repetitive choruses and are also well illustrated. Such books not only make learning to read easier, but also more inviting and worthwhile.

Building up a core of known narrative texts is essential to ensure children become acquainted with their rhythmic patterns and rhymes, and unconsciously begin to learn them by heart. Such tales may have formal story elements, and patterned openings and endings, for example:

- *In the light of the moon* (*The Very Hungry Caterpillar* by Eric Carle, Puffin)
- *In a dark dark wood* (*A Dark Dark Tale* by Ruth Brown, Red Fox)
- *Once upon a time* and *They all lived happily ever after* (traditional).

Such texts often provide clear models for mirrored stories, for example, 'We're Going on a Goblin/Fairy Hunt', based on '*We're Going on a Bear Hunt* by Michael Rosen (Walker Books), which can be acted out in drama or turned into a new class book. The language patterns can be borrowed and

repeated in shared writing activities and in children's own narratives, as can the rhymes, songs and choruses in texts, for example:

- *Run, run as fast as you can* ('The Gingerbread Man')
- *'Not now, Bernard,' said…* (*Not Now, Bernard* by David McKee, Red Fox)
- *'Tell us a story, Dad,' they said* (*Tell Us a Story* by Allan Ahlberg, Walker Books)
- *Little Rabbit Foo Foo riding through the forest* (Little Rabbit Foo Foo by Michael Rosen, Walker Books).

The more formal features of story language can be introduced through active reading sessions, recording favourite lines as in the activity 'Washing lines' and in the activities 'Songs, rhymes and chants', and 'Telling together'. Recommended repetitive rhythmic texts that children will enjoy include:

- *All Join In* – Quentin Blake (Red Fox)
- *Each Peach Pear Plum* – Janet and Alan Ahlberg (Puffin)
- *My Cat Likes to Hide in Boxes* – Eve Sutton (Puffin)
- *Knock Knock Who's There*? – Sally Grindley (Puffin)
- *Tell Us a Story* – Allan Ahlberg (Walker Books)
- *Out for the Count* – Kathryn Cave (Frances Lincoln)
- *Bearobics* – Vic Parker (Hodder Children's Books)
- *Tough Boris* – Mem Fox (Puffin)
- *The Fish Who Could Wish* – John Bush (OUP)

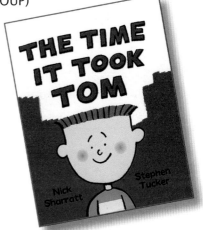

Book-spread

The purpose of this activity is to help children identify patterns in groups of text, either in the genre, for example, funny stories or animal stories, or in themes, such as love or loss. It can be undertaken with a small group or with the whole class. The activity also provides useful text recommendation opportunities, since the informal access to handling these books introduces children to titles they will later choose to read or re-read. Theme is not an easy concept at this age, but this work, if regularly undertaken, enables children to realise that books can be grouped into stories about different subjects or issues, such as books about being frightened, books about losing something, books about the dark, and so on.

Literature links

This activity utilises a range of texts in class, in book boxes or from the bookshelf. Try to make use of books that you know the children will have already met and know reasonably well. Include Big Books, guided reading sets, favourites from your read aloud time, as well as their own reading books. Picture books are more valuable than short novels in this activity, as a quick flick over the pages may remind the children of the storyline or at least enable them to see what the book is probably about.

What to do

❶ Invite the children to help you to create a 'book-spread' of your books. Tuck all the chairs in and take some time to spread the books over all the tables with their front covers facing upwards.

❷ Initially invite the children to walk around the tables until they find a book they have read, and give them some time to revisit and recall the storyline by looking at the illustrations.

❸ Ask the children to tell a nearby friend one thing they like about the chosen book, and to show them a picture from it. You may want to model this first by sharing a book you like with the class, pointing out your favourite picture and explaining why you like the book and that picture in particular. The focus here is not on theme but on favourite tales. Re-reading and revisiting these with a friend works as a warm-up to the activity and helps to re-acquaint the children with books in the class collection. The children may want to settle down on the floor for this part of the experience.

④ Choose a well-known Big Book and discuss with the class its theme. For example, *Owl Babies* by Martin Waddell (Walker Books) is about being separated from Mummy/the one we love – and being reunited with them.

⑤ Ask the children, in pairs, to look again at their chosen book and to decide on its theme. This might be growing up, families, being afraid of the dark, making friends and so on. Record a list of themes mentioned on a flipchart.

© Chris Kelly

⑥ Explain to the children that you would like to find out how many books there are in the class collection that have similar themes. Invite the children, in pairs, to go on a book hunt (not a bear hunt!) to find at least two books with a similar theme. They can either take their chosen book as the first one or they can start from scratch. Be sure to stress this is not a race.

⑦ Provide enough time for the children to hunt out books and to look at them to identify the theme. If you have put out well-known books this will not be as difficult as it sounds. Again they may wish to sit on the floor to read the books.

⑧ Ask the pairs of children to talk together about what the books they have collected have in common. You will need to model this first for them either with the Learning Support Assistant or with one of the children. The discussion should include a focus on the actual theme and also any other similar features, for example, how the stories both end happily, and so on. Some of the children may make lateral

connections to help fit texts together under certain themes. Accept these creative responses as it shows the children are thinking it through.

⑨ Let some of the pairs of children share their ideas and thoughts with the rest of the class.

Moving on

● Encourage the pairs to list their collected titles and authors under their own agreed headings. If done on strips of paper, these can be used to create a colourful wall display demonstrating the different themes available in the classroom.

● You might focus future book-spreads on characters or settings, asking the children to group texts with commonalities or contrasting features, or simply focus on likes and dislikes, author collections or illustrator piles.

Mirror the theme

© Chris Kelly

In 'Mirror the theme' children will be asked to use their understanding of themes of stories they know well in order to make intertextual links. The purpose of this activity is to support the children in identifying themes, discussing similarities with other texts and exploring differences. 'Telling news' may be a common occurrence in classrooms, but linking this with books and stories will lift the experience and provide it with more energy. Children will naturally link themes to their own experiences and will have much to offer to this kind of discussion. This is particularly so if they are focused on themes common to home and family life, for example getting lost, losing something, illness, the birth of a new baby, death, going on holiday or bullying.

What to do

❶ In preparation for this activity, make a collection of cards to represent common themes that can be found in the class story book provision, for example: being lost, a new baby, going away, getting into trouble, and so on. The cards can be simple images. Put these cards in a basket or container made especially for this activity and labelled 'Story themes'.

Literature links

There are innumerable examples from high quality picture books that will serve the purpose of this activity. All contain a meaningful story, rather than describing an incident as might be the case in a non-fiction text. Some useful examples might be: *This Is the Bear and the Scary Night* from the Sarah Hayes series (Walker Books), *Where's My Teddy?* by Jez Alborough (Walker Books), *Can't You Sleep, Little Bear?* by Martin Waddell (Walker Books) or *The Time It Took Tom* by Nick Sharratt and Stephen Tucker (Scholastic). This short list addresses themes including being lost, losing something, night-time fears and being in trouble at home.

❷ Initially, it is important to give the children an opportunity to browse among the class collection of books, preferably in pairs, with plenty of time to discuss the themes of stories they know well and to identify the themes in other stories they are less familiar with.

❸ Remind the children that information can be gathered from the image and title on the front cover of the book, a quick flick through the illustrations and the blurb on the back cover.

❹ Allow the children, one pair at a time, to pick, without looking, a card from the story themes basket and then to find a book or books that mirror this theme. If they are familiar with a number of the books already, then they will not find this task too difficult.

❺ Ask the children to read extracts from and discuss the book/s and to try to remember a time in their own lives when something similar happened to them or to someone they know.

❻ Model the activity on the first occasion, perhaps during shared reading time, by creating an anecdote to match a story

theme. Make the telling dramatic and embellish the story so that the children will imitate this style of storytelling, dramatising experiences and events in their own lives.

❼ Give the children time in pairs to tell their personal story.

❽ Using an A-shaped folded piece of card, so that each child can draw their story, ask them to represent simply in a single picture the theme of their experience, which could then be easily displayed with one or two books on the same theme.

Moving on

● Ask the children to create a title for their story that will represent its theme. They will need to look at the titles of other books as models for catchy, perhaps alliterative titles. The title could be independently written by the child or scribed by an adult. Create a display with the titles or use them as a classroom resource in the writing area.

● The book title resource could be used as an ongoing game for the children to play,

with one child selecting a title, for example 'Lost and Alone in Asda', and the other child required to name any other stories with a similar theme.

● Use pre-made stapled paper booklets to encourage the children to develop their own oral story into a book, drawn or written, that can then be used as part of the class book provision.

Speaking out

The aim of this activity is to encourage children to focus on the main character in a story, and to note relevant words and phrases and actions in order to work out the story's key theme. By examining the central character's behaviour and particularly speech, they will be able to identify the theme of the tale as it is expressed through the character's words and actions. Story themes are often presented in subtle ways, and young learners need to be offered a variety of techniques to access the different ideas and messages running through a story. In time, recognition and understanding of these techniques will help them to appreciate other stories more fully, and to use similar devices when contemplating how to develop themes in stories in their own writing.

Literature links

This activity suits stories in which the theme is explicitly or implicitly presented through the main character's words. Examples include the stories in this book, 'The Wrestling Animals' (page 90) – jealousy and arrogance, 'The Big Wide-mouthed Toad-Frog' (page 88) – learning when to talk and when to be quiet, and 'Sun Frog and Moon Frog' (page 92) – the consequences of not listening to our friends. Many traditional tales offer access to themes in this way, including 'The Three Billy Goats Gruff' and 'Little Red Riding Hood', as these have strong repetitive refrains which are an important feature of the structure of the text and reiterate the main theme. In the 'Three Billy Goats Gruff', each of the goats desires to cross the bridge and so they use their cunning to outwit the troll and get what they want. (*Oh no, you don't want me, my brother who is coming after me is larger and more juicy.*) Eventually, through their wit and determination they achieve their aim, even in the face of a serious obstacle. Some contemporary picture books will also be suitable for this activity. In stories with familiar settings, such as *A Baby for Grace* by Ian Whybrow (Kingfisher) and *You'll Soon Grow Into Them, Titch* by Pat Hutchins (Red Fox), the theme of being displaced by a sibling is conveyed, at least in part, by the main character's words.

What to do

❶ Retell or read a story to the class, for example, 'The Big Wide-mouthed Toad-Frog' or 'Sun Frog and Moon Frog' for more of a challenge. Encourage the children to join in with the two frogs' question and response conversations: *'Ribbit ribbit?' 'Ribbit ribbit.'* You and the children will need to work together to practise saying these with changing intonation as the action of the story develops and the actual meaning of the 'ribbits' changes.

❷ Explain to the group that you are going to read the story again and you want to focus on the main characters, Sun Frog and Moon Frog, and that you want the children to shake their heads every time one of the frogs speaks, as the frogs tend to do in the story. You could split the class into groups and allocate some of the frogs' other contented actions, to be mimicked at each speech, for example blinking, winking and even jumping.

❸ Start this second reading and each time the children shake their heads, blink or wink, chant the frogs' words together with a clear sense of intonation and inflection, to highlight the meaning behind those particular 'ribbits'. Write the phrases on the flipchart around sketches of the frogs. To help present the intonation, for example questioning or surprise or the usual disinterest, you could use capital letters, question marks and exclamation marks. Add other significant words from the story, for example, Rikki Tikki's *'Danger!'* If you are using 'The Big Wide-mouthed Toad-frog', for example, you could use upper-case letters for his words that are shouted and lower-case for the final whispered words when he comes across the alligator who eats Big Wide-mouthed Toad-Frogs.

❹ At the close of the story ask the children to re-read the frogs' words with you, noticing how the conversation at the end

of the story is in exactly the same tone as at the start.

❺ Give the children time to discuss, in pairs, what the theme of the story is. Add their suggestions, such as *trust, friendship, listening to advice* to the flipchart.

❻ From this, explain the theme of the story and how this has been shown through the main characters' attitudes and actions.

Moving on

● You could repeat the activity with another story, for example, 'Wee Meg Barnileg' (page 86). Encourage the children to make their own pictures of the main character and add their words and phrases based on her spoilt tantrums and later more apologetic stance. Together you could then discuss the theme as evidenced in her voice.

● 'Wee Meg Barnileg' could also be used as the basis for a class shared activity. Together, create a simple story about a creature who is afraid or bossy or mean, and learns not to be through a trip to the land of the 'faeries' like Meg.

Advertise the film

Video links

Depending upon their age, children will know and love the films below. It is a good idea to 'audit' the children for their favourite films and use them whenever you can. If you or the school do not own a copy of a particular title, you will probably be able to rent it. *Harry Potter and the Chamber of Secrets* (Warner), *The Jungle Book*, *The Little Mermaid* and *Finding Nemo* (all Disney) are always firm favourites. *Muppet Treasure Island* (Disney) is generally popular and so is *The Last Unicorn* (Carlton). *Bob the Builder – Knights of Can-A-Lot* (Hit Entertainment) is particularly good for younger children.

In this activity children learn how to employ persuasive language and to formulate a summary. The children are then challenged to inspire others to see a favourite film by describing the characters, action and themes. The activity uses a video box as a model. Children will be, for the most part, very familiar with watching videos and will be comfortable with the format of design and use of text on the box. This will help the children to comprehend more readily what you are asking them to do and to participate enthusiastically. Before you begin, make sure that the blurbs on your chosen video boxes use some of the simpler conventions of persuasive texts – for example, simple, present tense. First, the children are asked to consider how information for the video is conveyed through the wording and illustration on the box. Then they are encouraged to create their own description of a film, mimicking the language they have studied. Once the children are confident in the necessary skills, they can 'advertise' a film they are fond of to other children in the school.

What to do

❶ Choose a film that the children have seen either at school or at home. Ask the children to describe the cover illustration – it is often a picture of the main character. See if they can pick out and explain any other features on the box, for example the title, the filmmaker's name and the certificate the film carries. Draw the children's attention to the blurb on the back.

© Chris Kelly

❷ Now ask the children to tell you their favourite part of the film. Take three examples and then ask the children, in groups of three, to make a freeze-frame of the event that they found most memorable in the film. When they have planned it, ask all the children to hold their freeze-frame for you to inspect. Choose three groups to show the others what they were doing and ask the rest of the class to guess the scene.

❸ Once the children have returned to their seats, read them the blurb on the video box. Draw the children's attention to how the story is summarised. Concentrate on how language is used to encourage you to watch the film, pointing out relevant features, such as simple text structures and alliteration, for example: *The Jungle Book is a swingin' singin' song filled celebration you'll never forget.*

❹ Ask the children to recall their freeze-frames. What do they like about the film and why do they think others might like it too? Write notes on the board and construct a similar text using the children's ideas. Model the drafting process, crossing out, making changes and so on, as you go along.

Moving on

● You could ask the children to think of their favourite film and to make an advertisement for it based on the design and language of the blurb on the back of video boxes. They will need to illustrate their work and write using the features that you have emphasised. At this age, the children should be allowed to explore this genre for themselves and not restrict themselves to strict convention.

● You might wish to invite the children, with the support of their own advertisement, to orally advertise the film to other members of the class, or other classes.

CORNWALL COLLEGE
LEARNING CENTRE

Songs, rhymes and chants in stories

The aim of this activity is to develop children's awareness of songs, chants and rhymes in traditional tales and other stories. It celebrates the pleasure and patterns in such texts, and enables the children to notice, mark and memorise words through inventing and practising regularised physical actions to accompany them. Since the repeating patterns are frequently in the dialogue, for example: *'Ooh Grandma, what big ears you've got'* in 'Little Red Riding Hood' or, *'Little Rabbit Foo Foo, I don't like your attitude...'* (*Little Rabbit Foo Foo* by Michael Rosen, Walker Books), this activity also allows children to use rhymes and patterned language in stories as models for their own writing of narratives.

Literature links

Traditional tales employ many language patterns, rhythmic repetitions, songs and chants, for example, *The King with Dirty Feet and Other Stories* retold by Mary Medlicott (Kingfisher). However, there are many other picture books aimed at Early Years and Key Stage 1 which would also be suitable. A few good examples include, *My Cat Likes to Hide in Boxes* by Eve Sutton (Puffin), *Tell Us a Story* by Allan Ahlberg (Walker Books), *Each Peach Pear Plum* by Janet and Allan Ahlberg (Puffin), *Little Rabbit Foo Foo* by Michael Rosen (Walker Books), *Lullabyhullaballoo* by Mick Inkpen (Hodder Children's Books) and *The Grumpalump* by Sarah Hayes (Walker Books). The traditional tales in this book would be useful here too, especially 'The Big Wide-mouthed Toad-Frog' (page 88), 'Sun Frog and Moon Frog' (page 92) and 'How the Tides Came to Ebb and Flow' (page 94). You will know many other patterned and predictable texts which have strong choral refrains or chants for the children to join in with.

© Chris Kelly

What to do

❶ Read the beginning of a highly patterned story with regular refrains. Encourage the children to join in with the repeating words and phrases.

❷ Pause and agree on the voice intonation, volume and pace of the refrain. Practise it a couple of times, so the children are secure in the tenor and voice of it, then resume the story.

❸ Stop again, perhaps halfway through the narrative, and agree on some actions to go with the repeated words. These could be hand gestures, body movements, facial expressions, and so on. Ask the children for suggestions and practise the words and actions together so a regular and memorable pattern is set up.

❹ Complete the reading, employing these actions and the words in an exaggerated and marked manner throughout.

❺ Re-read the story, but this time perhaps the children could voice and act out the refrain without you joining in. They may be more reticent, but will gradually grow in confidence as the pattern sets in.

❻ Read the text again, but challenge the children to drop the words and keep the actions. You could hum the pattern of the words as a backdrop to their actions.

❼ In shared writing, borrow the repeating patterns from the story but change other elements. In 'The Big Wide-mouthed Toad-frog', for example, the Toad-frog could meet other creatures. He would ask the same question and always reply in the same way. Equally, Little Rabbit Foo Foo and the good fairy can carry on, whatever creatures the rabbit bops on the head!

> Old Woman, Old Woman Please listen to me!

> Fee-fi-fo-fum. I smell the blood of an Englishman.

> Hello! Hello! Hello! What are you and what do you eat?

> Who's been sitting in my chair?

Moving on

● You might want to write the refrain out on a large piece of paper, using clear spaces to indicate pauses, emboldened text for emphasis, and arrows, lines and signs to remind the class of the actions and intonation you created together. This could become a class poster to use when reading the book.

● Small groups of children could be invited to re-read the text themselves, with one taking the role of the narrator and the rest as the chorus. They could also make up their own physical actions for other texts and perform them to the class.

● The children could also create a display of texts with chants and repetitive vocal patterns and refrains and even add to this by bringing in books from home.

● You might try to make use of the exaggerated actions established for various stories as a five-minute guessing game. For example, you make the gestures, the class hum the pattern of the language and then together you identify the book and the author and revisit the refrain in words and actions through a re-reading of the tale.

'Get out of here'

This activity is based around an idea by Michael Rosen. It encourages children to make a direct link between speech and writing and shows them how their own voice can be 'heard' when presented on the page. We often look for ways to develop what has been called 'voice' in the children's writing. The voice of a piece of writing is when readers can hear the individuality of the writer in the words written down, almost as if they were talking to them face to face. Often we encourage children to concentrate too soon on the conventions of written language and sometimes that voice can begin to be blurred, even rubbed out. This activity attempts to retain that link directly. The activity also shows children that the writer can influence how a piece of writing should be read, by the way it is written down. This activity will lead on to discussions about the need for punctuation. Certain aspects of this activity will generate some noise, so you may need to warn those around you, but be confident that the children will be learning.

Literature links

Writers of children's books use a wide variety of devices to indicate the kind of reading they want. In *I Will Not Ever Never Eat a Tomato* and *I Am Not Sleepy and I Will Not Go to Bed* by Lauren Child (Orchard), the author employs different type fonts to suggest intonation. Poems, which are written to be performed, will often also help their readership in the same way, for example *Unzip Your Lips* chosen by Paul Cookson (Macmillan). *Hairy Tales and Nursery Crimes* by Michael Rosen (Collins) has the author up to his old tricks, engaging children by his devices for helping the reader.

from far far away

LEAPING AND BOUNDING

closer and **closer**

THE GHOST

SHOUTED

BOOOO!

Once I Was Coooooomeing home and I tripped over and then I Was Scared. Then my mum and dad heard it and they came running up the road and my dad picked me up. But then I didot feel sad. And when I got home I felt much better.

I Was on holiday at Dorset.
I could not wait to get to Dorset
when we got there I got
out of the car I fll and n.
and then my dad called me and then we all
went in the caravan.
We all had diner.
and when we where having diner there
was a massive.

loud
Storm
the End.

What to do

❶ Write *Get out of here* on the flipchart and ask the children to say this in as many ways as possible to the person sitting next to them, for example, as a question, as a command, slowly, quickly, loudly, with a hiss, and so on. This will be noisy, but great fun! You will probably have to model this for the children at first by trying some yourself, but it will not take long for the children to understand what they need to do.

❷ Now ask the children to write the words down in ways that reflect the different ways they have said them. This may mean using conventional punctuation and, for example, capital letters, but will also mean changing the size, extending the words by adding more letters, and so on. A slow but determined reading of the line may look like this: *Geeeeeeet ouuuuut offffffff herererererre!* Give some examples on the flipchart. Four different ways should do.

❸ Now ask the children to swap their writing with a neighbour and see if their partner can read the line in the intended manner. If not, discuss how the writing could be made more effective. What could the children do to make their reader read the text in the way they want? How can their voice be heard? Give them some time to discuss this in pairs and work on changing and re-reading.

Moving on

● Ask the children to tell their partners a short anecdote from their lives, for example: 'The scariest thing that has ever happened to me', 'The worst visit to the dentist', 'My recurring dream'. Ask the children to tell it in as expressive a way as possible. Then ask the children to write the story down in the way that they said it, using both conventional punctuation and the non-conventional devices they used with 'Get out of here'. This is great fun and illustrates the importance of retaining the 'voice' of the speaker in written versions. It is a challenge to do this, but is a splendid lesson in writing with the audience in mind.

● Encourage the children to ask their friends to read the story they have just written, to see if they have managed to use successful devices to enable the reader to read it as they intended. If they do not, the writer needs to go back to the text and make some changes. Stress to the children that this can be a difficult task, but that going back and changing writing is part of the creative process.

Washing lines

The purpose of this activity is to support the children as they begin to develop the language of stories as part of their active vocabulary. Children respond well to a multi-sensory approach to learning, and 'Washing lines' should be one activity among a variety of others, such as listening to commercial tapes of songs, rhymes and stories, and matching print texts. The children should have the opportunity to work in pairs, small groups and whole-class sessions to provide a varied learning experience. Displaying exciting vocabulary should be part of the creation of a rich and lively literacy environment, particularly at this Key Stage. From this the children can draw inspiration and also develop a sense of belonging to a community of writers who share, borrow and develop each other's ideas in the style of successful authors.

What to do

❶ The focus chosen for this activity will depend on the particular stage of the children's development and/or your current focus on literacy, for example, story openings or endings, rhymes, alliteration and so on. Although this activity could be introduced formally to the whole-class group to begin with, it should be part of the children's ongoing interest in language and literacy and therefore always available for further development.

❷ Select a story which is suitable for your chosen focus and then read the relevant section of the story to the children. If you are working on story openings, *Where's My Teddy?* by Jez Alborough has a particularly gripping sense of language and expression to raise a feeling of tension and anticipation.

In the dark dark town

the tall grass swished and whispered about them

She really was the teeniest tiniest mouse

Oi! Get off our train!

Literature links

This work could draw on the class collection of picture fiction, made available to the children through, for example, a book spread for this activity. Many recently published picture fiction texts will offer the range of vocabulary appropriate to this age group. Initially, however, the books could be pre-selected for the children to ensure that the focus vocabulary is contained in them. Stories, such as *A Dark, Dark Tale* by Ruth Brown (Red Fox) or *Where's My Teddy?* by Jez Alborough (Walker Books) provide straightforward opportunities to put this into practice.

❸ Talk to the children about, for example, in *Where's My Teddy?*, the significance of the beginning of stories, examining the language used, comparing it with other stories remembered, identifying particular words, phrases or devices that help to make us feel scared, interested or excited.

© Chris Kelly

❹ Identify with the children specific examples from the text that create atmosphere, for example: *He tip-toed on and on until...*

❺ Using one of the children's suggestions, write the phrase or sentence on a piece of card and peg it on a specially constructed line strung across a corner of the room or in the book area.

❻ Invite the children to browse among the rest of the book collection in the classroom to find other beginnings or phrases in stories that they like. Encourage them to discuss the reasons for their choices with another child in the class.

❼ Provide plenty of cards and felt-tipped pens so the children can add their personal favourite story phrases to the washing line.

❽ When the children have written their cards, share a few with the rest of the class. Identify which stories they have been taken from, and discuss with the children ways of grouping thes. For example, do they contain scary phrases, creepy words, cheerful beginnings, funny speeches or pretty descriptions?

❾ In a shared or guided writing session, invite the children to choose one or two 'washing-line words' to begin or include in a story opening.

❿ Small, informal, stapled booklets could be provided so that the children could continue writing their own story as an ongoing activity, either during independent time in the Literacy Hour or at other opportunities in the timetable.

⓫ Set aside time for these to be read aloud or included in the class book provision.

Moving on

● This should be an ongoing activity and will provide a useful writing resource for the class after the focus has moved on. The cards could be collected together in a basket or wall pouch, so that children can collect some ideas for inspiration when starting their own stories.

● The cards could also be used as an oral storytelling resource, with one child picking out a story opening and the rest of the class taking turns in a circle to continue it.

Telling together

Storytelling, whether based on personal stories or those from literature, needs to become a regular language practice in the primary classroom. It offers children the chance to retell powerful tales, to feel their tunes, use their patterns and rhythms and engage with their structures. Through retelling tales, children learn to creatively use their voice, face and hands, and find evocative language to spin their tale into existence as they engage their audience. A commitment to regular storytelling therefore ensures children are given opportunities to actively listen and respond to a range of stories told by different people, as well as to tell and retell stories themselves. In retelling, learners are able to lean on the structure of the known narrative and focus more upon the language of story. This activity involves a whole-class story circle, but small group storytelling can also be undertaken in a similar manner. Indeed, individuals and pairs can retell tales, perhaps for other classes, in a storytelling afternoon. The activity described here is quite simply a retelling in the class story circle. This supports the children in recalling the events of the tale and encourages them to make full use of some of the features of story language. Through repeated experience of telling stories, as well as reading them and hearing stories told and read, children begin to use more effective language in their written narratives. This is because they learn to borrow evocative lines and phrases, directly address the reader, and lean on the strong structures which inhabit the oral tradition.

A plethora of quality picture books, retellings and story tapes also exist which can help the teacher storyteller. These include *The Boy Who Lost His Bellybutton* by Jeanne Willis (Red Fox), *Chinye* by Obi Onyefulu (Frances Lincoln), *Bimwili and the Zimwi* by Verna Aardema (Hamish Hamilton), *What Made Tiddalik Laugh* by Joanna Troughton (Puffin) and *Anancy and Mr Dry-bone* by Fiona French (Frances Lincoln). In addition, short traditional tales are available in anthologies such as *South and North, East and West* edited by Michael Rosen (Walker Books) and *The King with Dirty Feet and Other Stories* edited by Mary Medlicott (Kingfisher) and *Cric.Crac. A Collection of West Indian Stories*

© Chris Kelly

retold by Grace Hallworth (Mammoth). The Society for storytelling (www.sfs.co.uk) offers a comprehensive list of taped tales or peruse the children's book review magazine, *Books for Keeps* (020 8852 4953), which reviews audiotapes as well. Be conscious in your selection, ensuring stories from many cultures are shared and try to avoid revisiting the popular western European fairy tales. There are a millennia of others to choose from, so try to work towards an appropriate balance over time.

Literature links

Traditional oral tales from many cultures abound, but be sure to select unknown narratives to tell, or the power of the texts to wonder and entertain is reduced. It will also help if there are repeated lines, phrases or actions. All of the tales given in this book come from the oral tradition and are probably better retold than just read to the class. 'Wee Meg Barnileg' (page 86), 'The Big Wide-mouthed Toad-frog' (page 88), 'The Wrestling Animals' (page 90) and 'How the Tides Came to Ebb and Flow' (page 94) all contain a clear narrative structure with a strong element of repetition which will help you recall the tale.

What to do

❶ Select a tale to tell, making sure it is one the class do not know. You will probably want to start by telling the story to yourself, to internalise its essence and remember its shape. You will also want to tell several others so that you feel at ease with the narrative prior to sharing it with your class. Make notes or draw pictures for yourself to aid memorisation, and practise the story to yourself and the cat (if you have one!), the mirror or members of your family in preparation. Begin to map out the structure of the story as a simple list of key words or phrases. Work out at which parts of the tale you will encourage the children to join in with your storytelling, either in simple actions or in words (often the repetitive runs are the easiest to mark through group involvement).

❷ Tell the children the tale, perhaps beginning with the chant, *Crick crack chin, my story's in* and ending with *Crick crack snout, my story's out,* and add some simple gestures to these words. These phrases will act as markers for the tale and can be taught to the children for their own use later. As you tell the story, model a variety of intonation patterns and gestures, using pace and pause to good effect. You can use your story notes, diagrams or pictures to help you.

❸ If you forget what happens next, say something like, *Crick crack snout, my story's partly out*, and ask the children to predict the next narrative event or share what they want to happen next with one another while you look at your notes. Continue the story and encourage the children to join in with any repetitive refrains and actions.

❹ Signal that you have finished telling the story and are back in your normal teacher role. Spend a few minutes with the children to share responses to the story. Together, create a simple visual representation of the first part of the tale on the flipchart.

© Derek Cooknell

❺ Rearrange the class so that you are all sitting in one circle. Provide an appropriate story object, for example, a small cloth frog for 'The Big Wide-mouthed Toad-frog', or a troll figure for 'The Three Billy Goats Gruff'. Begin the tale again, with everyone joining in the signal, *Crick crack chin, my story's in*. After you have told just the opening of the story, pass the object on to one of the the children sitting next to you and ask him or her to continue the story.

❻ As the object passes around the story circle, the child holding it retells the next small part of the tale. Each contribution may be very brief or more extensive, but stress to the children that you are all sharing the retelling of the tale. You may find that some of the children will need to take part twice as the story continues round (and round) the circle.

❼ As an individual follow-up task, ask the children to identify their favourite part of the tale and draw a picture with a couple of sentences to describe that chosen moment in the narrative. Focus on rich literary language and encourage the children to borrow phrases, lines, images and patterns from the tale.

Moving on

● Place the children's pictures in chronological order on a mural, which will become a large story journey showing the chosen tale. Fill in any gaps after discussion with the children.

● Ask the children to pair up, one as 'A' and one as 'B'. Restart the story, then pause and pass the telling space to all the 'A's in the room, who retell the next part of the narrative to their partner 'B'. After a short while, use a musical instrument to indicate that 'B' now has the telling space. Continue to swap the roles of teller and audience, until the tale is completed or, alternatively, take back the space yourself to conclude the tale.

● Encourage the children, in groups, to make storyboards of a tale you have told and then they can 'tell together' as a group, using the visuals to support their small group storytelling.

Stories to Tell

p86 Wee Meg Barnileg

p88 The Big Wide-mouthed
Toad-frog

p90 The Wrestling Animals

p92 Sun Frog and Moon Frog

p94 How the Tides Came
to Ebb and Flow

Wee Meg Barnileg

Years ago there lived a lass named Wee Meg Barnileg. I have to tell you that I've never met a child more spoilt than her, not in all my born days.

She was so fussy with her food: "Oh, I don't want that, I don't like that."

She was so particular about her clothes: "Oh, I won't wear that, I don't like that."

She was so rude about other people: "Oh look, Mummy, that girl's got no shoes."

She was not a popular child at all. Still, her parents doted on her; she was their only child and they spoiled her rotten.

Wee Meg was mean to animals too. Once, she poked a poor farm dog chained up in the hot sun and pulled his tail. The dog nipped her leg, and my, did Wee Meg Barnileg scream. Her parents came running. They fussed over her, but Meg only shouted at them that they should have come sooner.

One day Meg came upon a field where some men were working. Spying their bags packed with bread and cheese, Meg sat down and helped herself! Anything she didn't want she just tossed aside. In the warm sun she soon fell asleep.

When she awoke, she found night had fallen and a full harvest moon was gleaming in the sky. As she sat up she heard whispering voices. "That Meg Barnileg has ruined our midnight dancing. Look at all this food scattered over our ring."

Meg got to her feet and declared, "I didn't make the mess, it wasn't me…" She found herself in the middle of a ring of faeries. When they saw Meg, they joined hands and began to dance around her, singing:

Ring, ring, faerie ring,
Faeries dance and faeries sing.
Ring, ring, faerie ring,
Faeries dance and faeries sing.

Meg tried to step out of the circle, but she couldn't move a muscle. The faeries dragged her stiff body to a room underground piled high with wrinkled fruit, rotting bread and all manner of mouldy, half-eaten scraps.

"Do you see that?" said one of the faerie folk to Meg. "That's all the good food you've turned down and wasted in your life. You'll get neither a bite to eat nor a sup to drink till you've cleared it up."

Meg was furious. She complained bitterly, but the faerie folk stood firm. Meg's hunger got the better of her, so she gathered all the rotting rubbish and swept it into a pit. The faeries gave her a cup of milk and a crust of bread and so glad was Meg to get it that she didn't think to refuse.

Next the faieries took her to another room. On every surface lay piles and piles of old clothes – torn, grubby, crumpled clothes.

"Do you see that?" demanded a faerie. "Those are all the clothes you've tossed aside and never cleared up. You'll get neither a bite to eat nor a sup to drink till you've washed and ironed them all."

Meg was mad. She stamped her feet with fury, but the faerie folk stood firm. So Meg began to work. Her back ached from bending and her fingers throbbed from scrubbing, but at last the clothes were clean and pressed.

"Can I go home now?" she begged.

"No, you can't!" the faeries snapped. "There's more work to be done."

After another cup of milk and crust of bread, the faeries took her to a third room that was a mass of tangled weeds and thorns. Tiny flowers tried to show their heads.

"Oh the poor flowers," Meg cried, "they're being choked by all those weeds."

"Too right they are," agreed the faerie folk. "Those weeds are all the horrid things you've said about people and the flowers are the few nice words you've ever had to say. It's time to make amends, don't you think?"

Straight away, Meg began to pull out the weeds and release the flowers. As she worked, Meg pondered and pondered, and when she had finished, she apologised to the faeries for all the unpleasant things she had said and done.

With that, Meg found herself back in the faerie ring, up above the ground. The harvest moon was still gleaming and the faeries were still dancing. How was she going to get home? Then she remembered a story her gran had told her, and she searched the grass for a four-leafed clover. She seized one and, holding it tight, she made a wish. The next moment she was lying tucked up in her own bed at home!

Her mother was holding her hand, and called out in delight when Meg opened her eyes. Her father bounded upstairs. It turned out that Meg had been away with the faeries, unable to speak or move, for a year and a day.

From then on, Meg was a different daughter, a changed child. She was thankful for what she was given to eat, she kept her clothes clean and she always had a good word to say about everyone.

THE BIG WIDE-MOUTHED TOAD-FROG

Once, many moons ago, in a time even before our grandfathers were born, there lived two young people whose names were Jack and Mary. They were happy children and could often be found making dens to play in or climbing trees to watch from the treetops, as they enjoyed themselves in the great outdoors.

One day Jack said to Mary that if only they had a pet to join them, their life would be just perfect. So the pair set about making a trap, a 'trip-trap', to capture such a pet. It was neither too wide nor too deep, neither too rough nor too smooth and when their trip-trap was finished Jack declared that it was perfect.

"Perfect," agreed Mary and home they went to wait for morning.

On the morrow, Jack and Mary lifted the roof of woven willow branches from their trip-trap and peered inside. Lo and behold, what they saw before them was not very big and not very small. It was plump, wet, warty and green, with bright black eyes, long slimy legs and the biggest, widest mouth you've ever seen.

"Perfect," said Jack.

"Perfect," agreed Mary. "Our trip-trap has trapped a plump, wet, warty, green toad-frog and it's a Big Wide-mouthed Toad-frog at that!"

The perfect green frog hopped and skipped and jumped right out of the trip-trap and, landing on the grass beside them, he shouted, "HELLO! HELLO! HELLO! WHAT ARE YOU AND WHAT DO YOU EAT?"

"I'm Mary, and I like to eat cookies and chocolate and cakes and cheese."

"OOOH...! AAAH...! AMAZING...!" said the Big Wide-mouthed Toad-frog.

Then he turned to Jack. "HELLO! HELLO! HELLO! WHAT ARE YOU AND WHAT DO YOU EAT?" he demanded to know.

"I'm Jack, and I like to eat cookies and chocolate and caramel and carrots."

"OOOH...! AAAH...! AMAZING...!" repeated the Big Wide-mouthed Toad-frog loudly. "And now I must be off to explore the big wide world."

And with that the perfect green toad-frog hopped off down the road. Jack and Mary chased after him, but he was a perfectly determined frog and had soon disappeared into the rushes by the river.

The first strange creature that the Big Wide-mouthed Toad-frog met on his travels was a slender-legged, speckled animal with small branches growing out of its head. "HELLO! HELLO! HELLO! WHAT ARE YOU AND WHAT DO YOU EAT?"

"I'm a fawn. I eat grass, young shoots and green leaves," replied the young deer.

"OOOH…! AAAH…! AMAZING…!" shouted the Big Wide-mouthed Toad-frog, and he hopped and he skipped and he jumped on his way to more adventure.

The next amazing creature the Big Wide-mouthed Toad-frog met was an enormous animal, as large as a giant rock and covered with a rough fur rug. "HELLO! HELLO! HELLO! WHAT ARE YOU AND WHAT DO YOU EAT?" the Toad-frog demanded to know.

"Well, I'm a grizzly bear and I like to each fish and meat and honey and more fish and meat and honey."

"OOOH…! AAAH…! AMAZING…!" exclaimed the Big Wide-mouthed Toad-frog, and he hopped and he skipped and he jumped on his way to more adventure.

The third unusual creature the Big Wide-mouthed Toad-frog met on his travels had a bushy tail and a dark mask around his eyes, and it scampered across the ground in a very neat fashion. "HELLO! HELLO! HELLO! WHAT ARE YOU AND WHAT DO YOU EAT?" the Toad-frog demanded to know.

"I'm a racoon and I love to eat rotting rubbish and smelly leftovers," the fellow replied.

"OOOH…! AAAH…! AMAZING…!" exclaimed the Big Wide-mouthed Toad-frog, and he hopped and he skipped and he jumped on his way to more adventure.

Now the last creature the Big Wide-mouthed Toad-frog encountered looked like a long green log, with white roots glinting in the sunshine. "HELLO! HELLO! HELLO! WHAT ARE YOU AND WHAT DO YOU EAT?" he demanded to know.

"Well, heh-heh-heh, I'm an alligator and I just love to eat Big Wide-mouthed Toad-frogs," snarled the long green log. "Have you seen any here about?"

The Big Wide-mouthed Toad-frog looked into the dark eyes of the alligator and his big wide mouth grew smaller and smaller. He puckered his lips until they were tiny and he whispered, "I've not seen any Big Wide-mouthed Toad-frogs, not around here, not ever!"

Then the Big Wide-mouthed Toad-frog hopped and skipped and jumped, and he hopped and he skipped and he jumped all the way back to Jack and Mary's trip-trap. He became their pet and had many merry times with them, and they hopped and skipped and jumped round their garden together. The Big Wide-mouthed Toad-frog didn't travel far and he didn't keep asking questions, for he had learned an ever so important lesson: that sometimes it pays to keep your Big Wide Mouth SHUT!

THE WRESTLING ANIMALS

A long time ago there lived a prince who was very fond of all the animals in his kingdom. Every day, he went out riding through the forest to watch the animals living in their natural state. He saw Racoon living in a dirty burrow; he saw Polar Bear sleeping restlessly on freezing cold ice; he saw Tiger sweating away in the jungle and Zebra flicking his tale at the nasty little biting flies.

The way they lived made the prince sad, so one day he decided that he had to help at least one of them live in more comfort. He declared that he would ask one wild animal to come and live with him in his glorious palace. But which one? The prince thought long and hard, scratching his royal head.

"It's up to them," he said finally, "the animals will have to decide for themselves."

So, all the animals got together.

"Warm clean beds," yelped Racoon.

"Central heating," growled Polar Bear.

"The cool of air conditioning," roared Tiger.

"Power showers," whinnied Zebra.

The fact of the matter was they all wanted to live in the palace. There were other animals too who wanted to live there – Lion, Elephant, Wild Pig, Goat, Hyena and Cat.

The animals discussed and argued. "This is impossible," said Lion. "We will have to settle this by having a grand wrestling match."

The contest began with Elephant wrestling with Wild Pig. With his long strong trunk, Elephant swung poor Wild Pig around his head and threw him way off into the jungle.

Then Lion wrestled Elephant and scratched and bit him so hard on his trunk that Elephant went running into the forest, crying to his mother.

Then Lion wrestled with Goat, but Goat turned quickly, butting Lion up the bottom so he fell smack on his face and retired with a bloody nose.

The wrestling went on and on until only two animals were left: Hyena and Cat.

"This is going to be a cinch," laughed Hyena. "I'm a hundred times stronger than you."

Cat slowly licked her chops and stretched herself. "Well then, you wouldn't mind if we stepped outside?" she asked.

Hyena *was* much stronger than Cat, but each time he tossed Cat in the air, Cat fell back on her feet and sprang at Hyena again.

Hyena was getting fed up with this and screamed, "I'm the winner!"

"No you're not," said the other animals. "To win, you must either throw your opponent on their back or disable them so that they can no longer fight."

So Hyena tossed Cat time and time again, but each time Cat landed on her feet, ready for some more action. Hyena became so exhausted that eventually he rolled on his back and went fast asleep. Cat was declared the winner of the whole contest.

So Cat went to live with the prince. She could go wherever she wanted, enjoying all the wealth that the palace could provide. In fact she's still there, and when the prince talks to her she purrs softly or sometimes just stares with her beautiful frosty eyes.

Sun Frog and Moon Frog

In a time before our time began, when beasts did sing, birds did talk and grasshoppers did chew toffees, there lived two frogs: Sun Frog and Moon Frog. They dwelt happily on their lily pads, chatting merrily in the sunshine together.

"Ribbit Ribbit?"

"Ribbit Ribbit."

"Ribbit Ribbit?"

"Ribbit Ribbit."

They were great friends and could often be seen and heard doing what frogs are wont to do… Chatting: "Ribbit Ribbit?"

"Ribbit Ribbit…"

Staring… Glaring… Blinking… Winking… Jumping…

…and licking the air for flies: "Slurp, Gurgle, Slurp!"

One day, when the sun disappeared behind a mountain of cloud and the wind began to whistle and whine, Sun Frog and Moon Frog could still be heard…

"Ribbit Ribbit?"

"Ribbit Ribbit…"

Staring… Glaring… Blinking… Winking… Jumping…

…and licking the air for flies: "Slurp, Gurgle, Slurp!"

Just then they heard, "Rrrikki tikki, Rrrikki tikki, Rrrikki tikki." It was their friend, the Rikki Tikki bird, coming to visit them. She landed on Sun Frog's lily pad and whispered, "Danger, danger, danger!" in his ear.

He looked, shrugged his shoulders and shook his head. Yes, he shook his head!

So the Rikki Tikki bird hopped on to Moon Frog's lily pad and whispered, "Danger, danger, danger!" in her ear. But she too looked around, shrugged her shoulders and she shook her head. Yes, she shook her head.

The Rikki Tikki bird flapped her wings in frustration. Sun Frog looked at Moon Frog, and Moon Frog looked at Sun Frog, and they looked around, they shrugged their shoulders and they shook their heads, and continued in their usual way: "Ribbit Ribbit?"

"Ribbit Ribbit…"

Staring… Glaring… Blinking… Winking… Jumping…

…and licking the air for flies: "Slurp, Gurgle, Slurp!"

So the Rikki Tikki bird flew away. "Rrrikki tikki, Rrrikki tikki, Rrrikki tikki!"

Some time later, at twilight, Sun Frog and Moon Frog heard the first drops of rain fall into their pond, *plop-plop-plop!* The rain grew faster and fell more furiously, *plop-plop-plop! Plop-plop-plop! Plop-plop-plop!* The wind began to whistle louder and louder. Thunder clapped above them. Lightning flashed, *zigzag, zigzag, zigzag.*

Sun Frog looked at Moon Frog, and Moon Frog looked at Sun Frog, and they saw fear and trepidation in each other's eyes. They shook their heads. But they shook their heads in fear. The storm grew louder still; the rain fell in torrents, the wind moaned, thunder clapped and lightning snaked across the sky. As the terrifying storm reached its height, the two frightened frogs heard a familiar sound: "Rrrikki tikki, Rrrikki tikki, Rrrikki tikki!" It was the Rikki Tikki bird, come to rescue them.

"On my back," she squawked, "on my back." And the two frogs leaped upon the Rikki Tikki bird's back. She was forced to travel more slowly now, "Rrrikki—tikki, Rrrikki—tikki, Rrrikki—tikki!"

Their friend flew them three times around the world, until she spied a suitable new home for them. As Sun Frog and Moon Frog jumped off her back, they called their thanks to the Rikki Tikki bird:

"Ribbit Ribbit!"

"Ribbit Ribbit!"

And when she had gone, the two frogs settled down on their fresh green lily pads and could soon be seen and heard… chatting: "Ribbit Ribbit?"

"Ribbit Ribbit…"

Staring… Glaring… Blinking… Winking… Jumping…

…and licking the air for flies: "Slurp, Gurgle, Slurp!"

HOW THE TIDES CAME TO
EBB AND FLOW

Once in a place far from here, in a time when the Earth was new, an old woman had no hut to live in. She lived by the sea among the animals and birds. When the sun shone she was scorched, when the snow fell she was frozen, when the rain poured she was soaked, and when the winds whistled she was bitterly cold. Every day for as long as she could remember she had knelt and prayed to the great Sky Spirit To Whom All Things Belonged.

Sky Spirit, Sky Spirit
Please hear my prayer.
I'm alone and I'm homeless
And need you to care.

But the Sky Spirit, from his home in the heavens, always replied, "No home today: try again tomorrow," and the old woman was left without a home.

One day, however, the woman had a bright idea. She knelt and prayed to the great spirit in the sky:

Sky Spirit, Sky Spirit
Please hear my call.
I need a large rock
To give shelter to all.

The Sky Spirit, surprised by her unusual request, replied, "Take one, take one". A smile spread across the woman's face; her tired eyes twinkled; her worn body knew it would soon find rest. She knew exactly which rock she wanted, and so she rowed out into the ocean in her old stewpot. She rowed and rowed, and rowed and rowed, and soon who should she see but the Great Sea Bird, who cawed:

Old Woman, Old Woman
Please listen to me!
You are rowing too close
To the hole in the sea.

"Aha!" answered the old woman. "Then I think I am rowing the right way."
She rowed and rowed, and soon who should she see but the Little Rainbow Fish, who gurgled:

Old Woman, Old Woman
Please listen to me!
You are terribly close
To the hole in the sea.

"Aha!" answered the old woman. "Then I *know* I am rowing the right way."

At last her boat was becalmed. She peered down into the silent stillness and saw a rock more beautiful than any she had seen before. "That is the rock I want," she whispered, and she reached down towards it. But at that very moment the Sky Spirit To Whom All Things Belonged called to her from his home in the heavens:

> *Old Woman, Old Woman*
> *Now listen to me!*
> *DON'T take that rock*
> *From the hole in the sea.*

"But that's the rock I want," the old woman replied, and she reached down into the water. Then the Sky Spirit called again:

> *Old Woman, Old Woman*
> *Are you listening to me?*
> *Surely you're not taking*
> *The rock from the sea!*

"But that's the rock I want," the old woman insisted, and she reached down deeper into the water. Then the Sky Spirit called a third time:

> *Old Woman, Old Woman*
> *You're not listening to me;*
> *I'm telling you, DON'T*
> *Take the rock from the sea!*

"But you said I could take one!" the clever woman replied. She pulled and she heaved until *Sssloop…!* Out came the rock from the ocean floor. Then the Sky Spirit was sorry; the waters poured down and down through the hole in the sea.

The sea glugged and gurgled, and sucked and swirled and twisted around faster and faster as all the water of the oceans rushed towards the hole. The old woman's stewpot was tossed in circles, but she held on tight to the rock.

"Put it back!" cried the Great Sea Bird and the Little Rainbow Fish and all the creatures of the air and the sea who were terribly afraid.

"Put it back!" roared the furious Sky Spirit, gathering the thunderclouds.

But the old woman refused to put it back. "It's mine now," she called to them.

So the Sky Spirit sent Little Dog down to Earth: "Go with haste, Little Dog, and put your nose in the hole in the sea."

Little Dog did as he was told, but his nose was too small and the water so cold. The oceans continued to pour through the hole, *slurrsh, slurrsh, slurrsh,* and Little Dog swam to the surface.

The old woman took him into her stewpot and said, "From now on you will be my little dog, and I will love you always."

So the Sky Spirit sent Young Maiden down to Earth: "Go with haste, Young Maiden, and kneel in the hole in the sea."

Young Maiden did as she was told, but her knees were too thin and the water so cold. The oceans continued to pour through the hole, *slurrsh, slurrsh, slurrsh,* and Young Maiden swam to the surface.

The old woman took her into her stewpot and said, "From now on you will be my daughter, and I will love you always."

In desperation the Sky Spirit sent Young Man down to Earth: "Go with haste, Young Man, and sit in the hole in the sea."

Young Man did as he was told, but still the hole was too big and the water so cold. The oceans poured relentlessly through the hole, *slurrsh, slurrsh, slurrsh,* and Young Man swam to the surface.

The old woman took him into her stewpot and said, "From now on you will be my daughter's husband, and I will love you always."

Just then, the waters swirled faster, and the stewpot was tossed towards the hole. "Put back the rock!" cried all the creatures of the air and the sea.

"*Please* put back the rock," cried the Sky Spirit. "I will let you borrow it twice a day."

The ancient old woman looked at Little Dog who would love and protect her, at Young Maiden who would talk to her, and at Young Man who would build her a hut, and she smiled. She reached over the side of the stewpot and replaced the rock in the hole in the sea, *phut!*

The waters stilled, the sea filled up, and the contented old woman rowed home with her new family. From that day to this, the old woman has borrowed that rock twice a day to pretty up her garden. As she removes the rock, the water goes down and down into the hole in the sea. When she replaces the rock, the sea fills up. That is why the tides ebb and flow.

But some parts of Little Dog, Young Maiden and Young Man never did warm up. To this day all dogs have cold noses, all maidens cold knees and all young men stand with their backs to the fire.